Collins

INTERNATIONAL PRIMARY MATHS

Workbook 3

William Collins' dream of knowledge for all began with the publication of his first book in 1819. A self-educated mill worker, he not only enriched millions of lives, but also founded a flourishing publishing house. Today, staying true to this spirit, Collins books are packed with inspiration, innovation and practical expertise. They place you at the centre of a world of possibility and give you exactly what you need to explore it.

Collins. Freedom to teach.

An imprint of HarperCollins*Publishers*
The News Building
1 London Bridge Street
London
SE1 9GF

Browse the complete Collins catalogue at
www.collins.co.uk

10 9 8

ISBN 978-0-00-815990-0

British Library Cataloguing in Publication Data
A catalogue record for this publication is available from the British Library.

Commissioned by Fiona McGlade
Series editor Peter Clarke
Project editor Kate Ellis
Project managed by Emily Hooton
Developed by Joan Miller, Tracy Thomas and Karen Williams
Edited by Catherine Dakin
Proofread by Catherine Dakin
Cover design by Ink Tank
Cover artwork by Jose Lis Petaez/Getty Images
Internal design by Ken Vail Graphic Design
Typesetting by Ken Vail Graphic Design
Illustrations by Ken Vail Graphic Design, Advocate Art and Beehive Illustrations
Production by Lauren Crisp

Printed and bound by Grafica Veneta S. P. A.

Contents

Number

Geometry

Measure

Handling Data

Number

Lesson 1: **Reading and writing numbers**

- Count to 200 and beyond
- Read and write numbers to 1000

Challenge 1

1 Write these numbers in numerals.

a twenty-nine ☐   **b** forty-seven ☐

c ninety-one ☐   **d** sixty-four ☐

e fifty ☐   **f** thirty-eight ☐

2 Count on from each of these numbers.

a 134, 135, 136, ☐ , ☐ , ☐ , ☐

b 177, 178, 179, ☐ , ☐ , ☐ , ☐

Challenge 2

1 Draw a line to match each number written using numerals with the number written in words.

589 •   nine hundred and fifty-eight

598 •   eight hundred and fifty-nine

958 •   five hundred and eighty-nine

580 •   nine hundred and five

859 •   five hundred and ninety-eight

905 •   five hundred and eighty

2 Write each number in words and then in numerals.

a 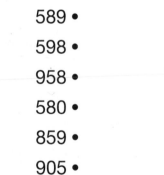 [_____] ☐

b [_____] ☐

c [_____] ☐

2

d

e

f

3 Use these word cards to make four different 3-digit numbers.
Write your numbers in numerals.

fifty

two

hundred and

seven

thirty

a

b

c

d

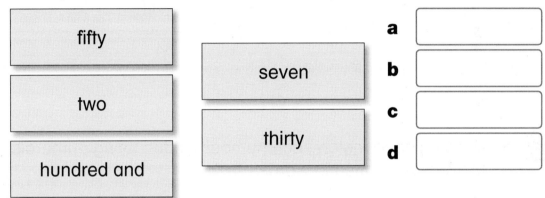

Challenge 3 Use the numbers on the digit cards to make five different 4-digit
numbers. Then write your numbers in words.

6   0   5   2   9

a

b

c

d

e

3

Number

Lesson 2: **Counting on and back in steps (1)**

• Count on and back in 1s, 10s and 100s

Challenge 1

1 Write the number in each box as you count in 1s.

a 53, 54, ☐, ☐, 57, ☐, ☐

b 87, ☐, 89, ☐, ☐, ☐, 93

2 Write the number in each box as you count in 10s.

a 14, 24, ☐, 44, ☐, ☐, ☐, 84

b 28, ☐, ☐, ☐, 68, ☐, 88

c ☐, ☐, 53, 63, ☐, ☐

Challenge 2

1 Count in 1s.

a 4 2 5, ☐, ☐, ☐, ☐

b ☐, ☐, ☐, 3 6 1, ☐

2 Count in 10s.

a ☐, ☐, ☐, ☐, 7 2 9

b ☐, 5 8 1, ☐, ☐, ☐

3 Count in 100s.

a [2 0 6] , [ ] , [ ] , [ ] , [ ]

b [ ] , [ ] , [6 9 3] , [ ] , [ ]

4 Jaden thinks of a number and counts in 100s for four steps.
  He ends on the number 792.
  What number did he start with? [ ]

5 Max counts in 10s from the number 85. Circle the numbers that he will **not** say.

  105   147   125   231   485

6 Amira counts back in 10s for five steps. She ends on the

  number 380. What number did she start on? [ ]

Challenge 3

1 Count in 100s from 179 to 879. Not counting 179, how many numbers do you say?

  [ ]

2 Count in 10s from 242 back to 52. Not counting 242, how many numbers do you say?

  [ ]

3 You counted back to 370 in tens. You have said 8 numbers. What was your starting number?

  [ ]

5

Lesson 3: **Counting on and back in steps (2)**

Number

- Count forwards and backwards in 2s, 3s, 4s and 5s

 Challenge 1

1 Join the numbers in order, counting in 2s, to form a sequence.

2   12   8   10
  6   4   14

2 Join the numbers in order, counting in 5s, to form a sequence.

5   15   10   35
  20   30   25

 Challenge 2

1 Complete each sequence.

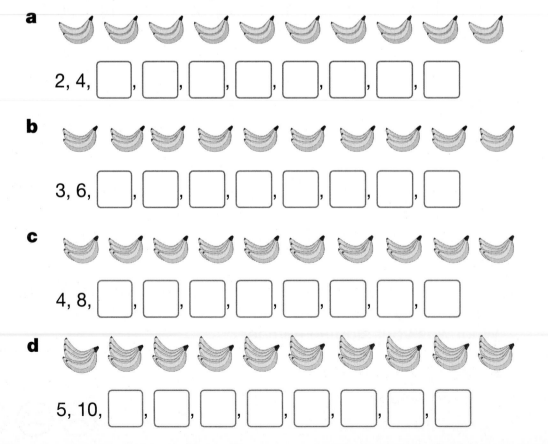

a   2, 4, ☐, ☐, ☐, ☐, ☐, ☐, ☐, ☐

b   3, 6, ☐, ☐, ☐, ☐, ☐, ☐, ☐

c   4, 8, ☐, ☐, ☐, ☐, ☐, ☐, ☐

d   5, 10, ☐, ☐, ☐, ☐, ☐, ☐, ☐

2 a Meera counts in 3s from 27. Colour the numbers she says.

(39)   (31)   (43)   (45)   (37)

b She counts back in 5s from 50. Colour the numbers she says.

(26)   (35)   (50)   (48)   (40)

c She then counts in 4s from 24. Colour the numbers she says.

(48)   (27)   (30)   (36)   (31)

d Meera counts back in 4s from 40. Colour the numbers she says.

(35)   (28)   (23)   (20)   (16)

Challenge 3

Start at 24 and count on in 2s. Draw a red stripe through each number you say.

1	2	3	4	5	6	7	8	9	10
11	12	13	14	15	16	17	18	19	20
21	22	23	24	25	26	27	28	29	30
31	32	33	34	35	36	37	38	39	40
41	42	43	44	45	46	47	48	49	50

Start at 12 and count on in 3s. Draw a blue stripe through each number you say.

Start at 20 and count on in 4s. Draw a yellow stripe through each number you say.

Start at 15 and count on in 5s. Draw a green stripe through each number you say.

a Do any numbers have four stripes? _____

b Which numbers have three stripes?

7

Lesson 4: **Place value (1)**

• Recognise the value of each digit in a 3-digit number

 Write the 3-digit number made by the Base 10 equipment.

a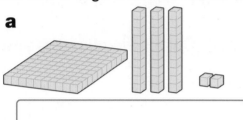

b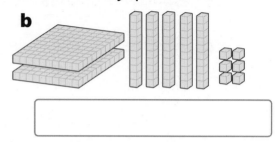

 1 Look at each target board. What number is being shown?

a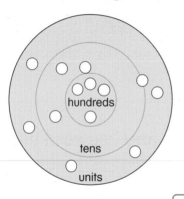

b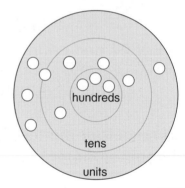

c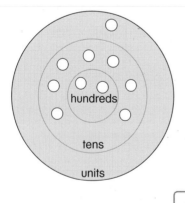

d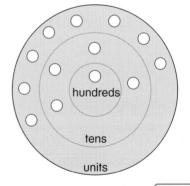

e Which of the numbers has a digit 2 that is worth 2 tens (or 20)?

f Which of the numbers contains a digit 1 that is worth 1 hundred (or 100)?

2 Joseph makes different totals using the target. How does he make them?

Example: 248 = 2 hundreds + 4 tens + 8 units

a 647 = ☐ hundreds + ☐ tens + ☐ units

b 357 = ☐ hundreds + ☐ tens + ☐ units

c nine hundred
and forty-nine = ☐ hundreds + ☐ tens + ☐ units

d seven hundred and thirty-three
= ☐ hundreds + ☐ tens + ☐ units

e Which of Jacob's scores has the same number of hundreds and units? ☐

 Challenge 3 You have four number cards. You can only use each one once in the same number.

6 2 4 1

a What is the smallest 3-digit number you can make from the cards? ☐

b What is the largest 3-digit number you can make? ☐

c Make a 3-digit number with an odd number of 10s. ☐

d Make a 3-digit number in which the 100s digit is worth twice as much as the 10s digit. ☐

Lesson 5: **Place value (2)**

- Recognise the value of each digit in a 3-digit number
- Partition 3-digit numbers into hundreds, tens and units

 Challenge 1 What is the value of each digit in these numbers?

a
348

b
273

 Challenge 2 **1** Each fork shows a 3-digit number. Write the number under the fork, then draw a line from each number to the description that matches.

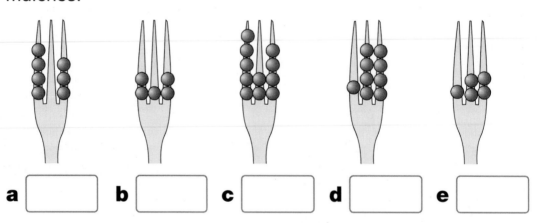

a [ ] **b** [ ] **c** [ ] **d** [ ] **e** [ ]

> The largest number shown.

> A number in which the digit 2 is worth 2 hundreds.

> The smallest number shown.

> An odd number.

> A number with 4 tens.

2 Asim uses peas on a fork to make these 3-digit numbers. Write how each number can be split up.

Example: 914 = 900 + 10 + 4

a 532 = ☐ + ☐ + ☐   **b** 245 = ☐ + ☐ + ☐

c 781 = ☐ + ☐ + ☐   **d** 386 = ☐ + ☐ + ☐

d three hundred and fifty-nine = ☐ + ☐ + ☐

e four hundred and sixty = ☐ + ☐ + ☐

f Which of Asim's numbers has no tens? ☐

Challenge 3 You have only 9 beads.

Draw 9 beads on each abacus to answer each question.

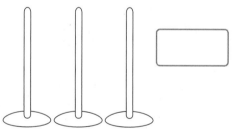   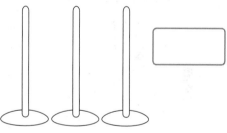

a What is the largest 3-digit number you can make?

b What is the smallest 3-digit number you can make?

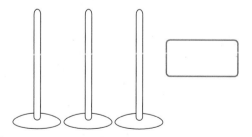   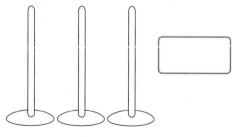

c Make a 3-digit number in which the 4 is worth 4 hundreds.

d Make a 3-digit number in which the number of tens is the same as the number of units.

Number

Lesson 6: **1, 10, 100 more or less (1)**

• Find 1, 10 or 100 more or less than a number

Challenge
1

1 Write the number that is 1 more than:

a 58 ☐   **b** 43 ☐   **c** 121 ☐

d 142 ☐   **e** 287 ☐   **f** 108 ☐

2 Write the number that is 10 less than:

a 85 ☐   **b** 29 ☐   **c** 153 ☐

d 184 ☐   **e** 197 ☐   **f** 216 ☐

Challenge
2

1 These are all parts of different number squares. Fill in the numbers that are 1 and 10 more and less.

	372	
381	**382**	383
	392	

a 184

b 235

c 429

d 763

e 557

f 846

2 a Write the missing numbers in the table.

100 less				
	348	679	109	855
100 more				

b Look at your answers in the table above. Which part of these numbers change as you find 100 less and 100 more?

_____

_____

3 Write the missing numbers in the table.

1 less				
	793	500	897	300
10 more				

Challenge 3

1 Rosie thinks of a number. She finds 100 more than her number. Her answer is 821. What was the number she thought of?

2 Rosie thinks of another number. This time she finds 10 less than her number. Her answer is 694. What was the number she thought of?

3 Rosie thinks of a 3-digit number in which two of the digits change when she finds 1 more than her number. Write five different numbers it could be.

13

Number

Lesson 7: **Marking numbers on a number line (1)**

- Place 3-digit numbers on a number line marked in multiples of 100

Challenge 1 What number do you think each blank T-shirt represents?

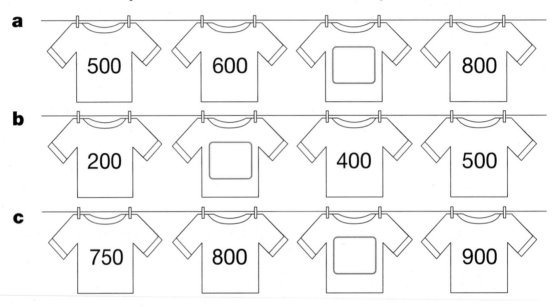

a 500 600 ☐ 800

b 200 ☐ 400 500

c 750 800 ☐ 900

Challenge 2

1 On each number line, write two numbers in the correct places.

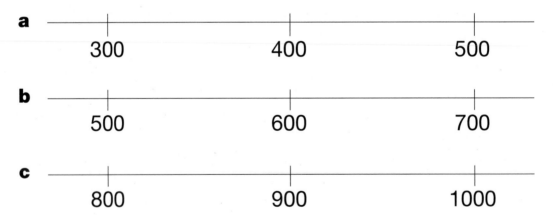

a 300 400 500

b 500 600 700

c 800 900 1000

2 Which numbers are being shown on this number line?

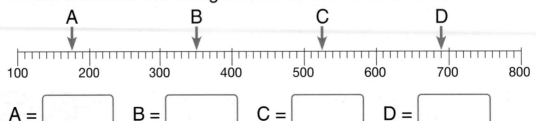

A   B   C   D

100   200   300   400   500   600   700   800

A = ☐   B = ☐   C = ☐   D = ☐

14

3 Draw lines to show where these numbers belong on the number line.

482 158 720 921 399

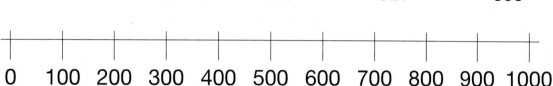

1 Kwame makes three different numbers out of the same three digit cards.

This is where each number belongs on a number line.

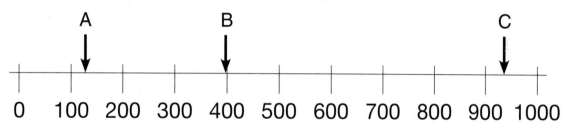

What numbers did Kwame make?

A = ☐ B = ☐ C = ☐

2 Kwame takes three new digit cards and makes three new numbers.

This is where each number belongs on a number line.

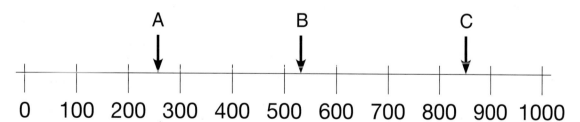

What numbers did Kwame make?

A = ☐ B = ☐ C = ☐

☹ 😐 ☺

Lesson 8: **Marking numbers on a number line (2)**

* Place 3-digit numbers on a number line marked in 10s

Challenge 1

Draw an arrow to show where the number belongs on the number line.

a 83

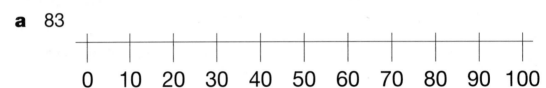

b 42

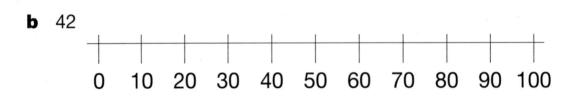

c 158

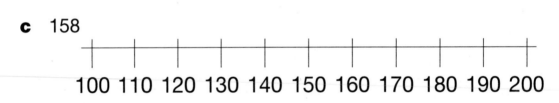

Challenge 2

1 Draw an arrow to show where the number belongs on the number line.

a 254

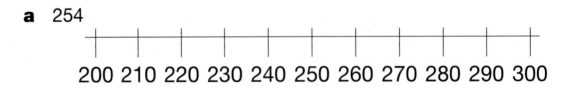

b 381

c 648

Number

2 Write a number that each letter could point to.

A = [   ]   B = [   ]   C = [   ]   D = [   ]

Challenge 3

1 Ella uses the same digits to make two 3-digit numbers.

The first lies between 710 and 720 on a number line.

The second lies between 770 and 780 on a number line.

Work out what Ella's numbers must be and then write them on this number line.

First number = [   ]   Second number = [   ]

2 Ella chooses three different digits. She makes two new 3-digit numbers between 300 and 400.

The first is greater than 390.

The second is less than 320.

Work out what Ella's numbers must be and then write them on this number line.

First number = [   ]   Second number = [   ]

Number

Lesson 1: Counting on and back in steps (3)

• Count on and back in different-sized steps

1 Each of these frogs jumps in 1s. Fill in the missing numbers.

a

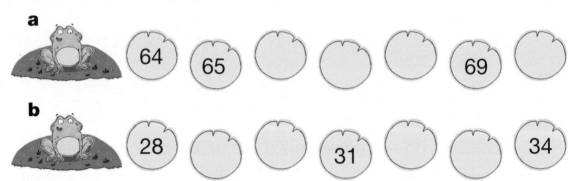

64 65 ◯ ◯ ◯ 69 ◯

b

28 ◯ ◯ 31 ◯ ◯ 34

2 Each of these frogs jumps in 10s. Fill in the missing numbers.

a

47 57 ◯ ◯ ◯ 97

b

◯ ◯ 55 65 ◯ ◯

1 Ashia is counting in 1s, 10s and 100s.

a She starts from 146 and counts on in 1s to 151.
Write out the numbers she says.

b She starts from 449 and counts back in 10s to 399.
Write out the numbers she says.

c She starts from 302 and counts on in 100s to 802. Write out the numbers she says.

2 a Colour the numbers Ashia says if she counts back in 100s from 739.

| 239 | 839 | 729 | 139 | 639 | 939 |

b Colour the numbers Ashia says if she counts on in 10s from 294.

| 382 | 304 | 354 | 254 | 234 | 364 |

3 Ashia says that if she counts forward from 527 in 10s, every number will be an odd number.

Is she right? Yes / No

Explain your answer.

_____

_____

Challenge 3

1 Jared counts backwards in 10s six times. He ends up on the number 739. What number did he start with?

2 Jared counts forwards in 100s five times. He ends up on the number 802. What number did he start with?

3 Jared counts backwards in 1s three times. He ends up on an even number with five 100s and two 10s. What number could he have started with?

☹ 😐 ☺

19

Lesson 2: **Place value (3)**

Number

• Know the value of each digit in a 3-digit number

Challenge 1 Circle the number in which...

a	...the 8 is worth 8 tens	389	893	938
b	...the 3 is worth 3 hundreds	543	435	354
c	...the 1 is worth 1 unit	821	812	182
d	...the 0 is worth 0 tens	930	390	309
e	...the 2 is worth 20	642	264	426
f	...the 6 is worth 600	613	361	136

Challenge 2 1 Write down the number that you could make from these place value cards.

a   400   20   5

b   600   30   8

c   800   10

d   100   7

e   200   80

f   500   4   90

g   9   300   50

Number

2 Complete each set of place value cards to show how to make the number.

a 254 =

b 872 =

c 944 =

d 587 =

Challenge 3

1 Write down a 3-digit number that fits the clues.

a An even number with 6 hundreds

b A number with the same amount of tens and units

c A number where a 2 digit is worth 20

2 Olivia has the following digits:

a What is the largest 3-digit number she can make with these digits?

b Write a 3-digit number Olivia can make in which the digit 8 is worth 8 tens.

c What is the smallest 3-digit number Olivia can make?

Lesson 3: **1, 10, 100 more or less (2)**

• Find 1, 10 or 100 more or less than a number

Challenge 1

These are all parts of different number squares. Fill in the numbers that are 1 and 10 more and less.

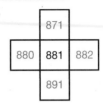

```
          871
      880 881 882
          891
```

a

249

b

453

c

782

d

156

Challenge 2

1 Write down how to change each of these numbers.

Example: 304 to 294 | 10 less

a 482 to 483

b 332 to 232

c 702 to 712

d 573 to 673

e 900 to 899

f 201 to 191

g 495 to 505

h 888 to 788

2 Mark the jumps on the number lines.
   Example: 10 more than **629**

600   629 639   700

a 10 less than **483**

400   500

b 100 more than **715**

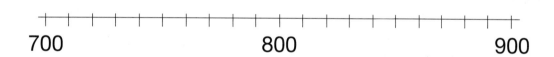

700   800   900

c 1 less than **845**

840   850

d 10 more than **291**

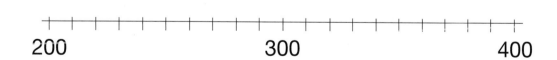

200   300   400

Challenge 3

1 A grasshopper is on the number 529. It makes
   3 different jumps of 1, 10 and then 100.
   Can it land on the number 618?

2 Sahir chooses a mystery number, then counts
   100 more than it. His new number is 312.
   What was his mystery number?

Number

Lesson 4: **Multiplying by 10 (1)**

* Multiply 2-digit numbers by 10

Challenge 1

Draw a line to match each calculation with its answer.

8 × 10   12 × 10

4 × 10   150   40   120   15 × 10

10 × 10   16 × 10

80   160   100

Challenge 2

1 Show how each number shifts to the left when it is multiplied by 10.

Example: 39 × 10

H	T	U
	3	9

× 10 →

H	T	U
3	9	0

a 84 × 10

H	T	U

× 10 →

H	T	U

b 96 × 10

H	T	U

× 10 →

H	T	U

c 50 × 10

H	T	U

× 10 →

H	T	U

d 13 × 10

H	T	U

× 10 →

H	T	U

e 60 × 10

H	T	U

× 10 →

H	T	U

f 61 × 10

H	T	U

× 10 →

H	T	U

2 Complete these calculations

a 64 × 10 = ☐   **b** 91 × 10 = ☐

c 17 × 10 = ☐   **d** 28 × 10 = ☐

e 35 × 10 = ☐   **f** 14 × 10 = ☐

3 This machine multiplies numbers by 10. Complete the tables.

IN	OUT
47	
88	
	750
	420
19	
	200
32	
99	

Challenge 3 George takes four different digit cards.

He uses them to make two different 2-digit numbers.

He then multiplies the numbers he makes by 10.

His answers are 730 and 210.

a What are his digit cards?

☐ ☐ ☐ ☐

b Write four more × 10 calculations with George's digits.

☐ ☐

☐ ☐

Number

25

Number

Lesson 5: **Rounding**

• Round 2-digit and 3-digit numbers

You will need
• coloured pencils

Challenge 1

1 Colour the numbers that round to 70.

(64) (68) (71) (69) (73) (76)

2 Colour the numbers that round to 30.

(31) (29) (24) (37) (25) (38)

3 Colour the numbers that round to 90.

(95) (87) (85) (93) (91) (82)

4 Colour the numbers that round to 20.

(28) (24) (15) (17) (12) (22)

5 Colour the numbers that round to 50.

(52) (53) (44) (58) (45) (55)

Challenge 2

1 Mark each number on the number line. Show whether you would round it up or down, to the nearest 10.

Example: 67

60   67 70

a 89

80   90

b 54

50   60

c 65

60   70

d 32

30   40

2 Mark each number on the number line. Show whether you would round it up or down to the nearest 100.

Example: 326

300 326   400

a 858

800   900

b 520

500   600

c 489

400   500

d 150

100   200

e 714

700   800

f 349

300   400

Challenge 3 Keisha says: 'If I add the digits of my mystery number, they make 14. If I round my mystery number to the nearest 100, it rounds to 500.'

What could Keisha's number be?

Invent a similar puzzle of your own for a friend to try.

Number

Lesson 6: **Comparing numbers (1)**

• Use > and < signs to compare 3-digit numbers

Challenge 1

1 Complete each sentence to show what the symbol means.

  a The < symbol means 'is _____ than'.

  b The > symbol means 'is _____ than'.

2 Mark each comparison with a tick (✓) or a cross (✗) to show whether it is right or wrong.

  a 84 > 74 ☐   **b** 37 > 39 ☐

  c forty-nine < 67 ☐   **d** 82 < 81 ☐

  e 95 > eighty-five ☐   **f** sixty < 82 ☐

Challenge 2

1 Write the correct symbol (> or <) between each pair of numbers.

  a 145 ☐ 154   **b** 734 ☐ 347

  c 628 ☐ 286   **d** 289 ☐ 298

  e 703 ☐ 730   **f** 294 ☐ 249

  g 101 ☐ 110   **h** 487 ☐ 478

  i 529 ☐ 295   **j** 422 ☐ 242

2 Shona makes these statements comparing 3-digit numbers. Write out her comparisons, using only digits and symbols.

  a Three hundred and twelve is more than three hundred and two.

  ☐

  b Seven hundred and eight is less than eight hundred and seventy.

  ☐

c Five hundred and forty-four is more than four hundred and fifty-nine.

3 Write a 3-digit number that makes each comparison true.

a 295 < ⬜

b 402 > ⬜

c 772 > ⬜

d 266 < ⬜

e 834 > ⬜

f 333 > ⬜

4 Write a 3-digit number that lies between the numbers shown.

a 348 ⬜ 386

b 579 ⬜ 597

c 433 ⬜ 455

d 110 ⬜ 144

 Challenge 3

Shona and Kyle are playing a game.

Kyle makes a number out of three digit cards and writes a symbol.

Shona then has to rearrange Kyle's cards to make a different number that makes the comparison true.

Can you help her? Remember that each statement must be true.

Example: 4 5 9 < 9 5 4

a 6 2 5 < ⬜⬜⬜

b 1 9 2 > ⬜⬜⬜

c 8 3 4 < ⬜⬜⬜

d 5 0 2 < ⬜⬜⬜

e 9 2 5 > ⬜⬜⬜ or ⬜⬜⬜

f 3 1 8 < ⬜⬜⬜ or ⬜⬜⬜

☹ 😐 ☺

Number

Lesson 7: **Ordering numbers (1)**

• Order 2- and 3-digit numbers

Draw a circle around the largest number in each set. Draw a square around the smallest number in each set.

a	38	49	18	48	39
b	25	15	19	35	20
c	93	99	95	97	98
d	57	50	75	77	55
e	49	52	60	57	59

1 These tickets show the order people need to be seen in a doctor's surgery. Write each set of tickets in order, smallest to largest.

a

> 78 > 47 > 21 > 39

> > > >

b

> 30 > 94 > 52 > 13

> > > >

c

> 26 > 23 > 75 > 59

> > > >

d

> 384 > 834 > 348 > 438

> > > >

e

> 619 > 691 > 196 > 916 > 169

> > > > >

f

> 527 > 275 > 725 > 257 > 572

> > > > >

2 These are the ticket numbers of people standing in a queue.

One person is in the wrong place. Circle the wrong number and then write out each list correctly.

a 832, 853, 835, 849, 852

b 409, 410, 437, 421, 439

c 571, 517, 538, 565, 569

3

> The best way to compare 3-digit numbers is to compare the hundreds digit first, then the tens, then the ones.

Adil

Josh

> That's not right! You always need to start with the ones.

Who is right and why?

_____

_____

Challenge 3 Complete each list so that the 3-digit numbers are in order, smallest to largest.

You are only allowed to use each digit once in each of the numbers in the row.

0 1 2 3 4 5 6 7 8 9

a 5 ▢▢ , 5 ▢▢ , 5 7 3, 5 ▢▢ , 5 ▢▢

b 2 ▢▢ , 2 6 4, 2 ▢▢ , 2 ▢▢ , 2 ▢▢

c 7 ▢▢ , 7 ▢▢ , 7 ▢▢ , 7 ▢▢ , 7 6 8

Number

Lesson 8: **Estimating**

You will need
• exercise book

• Estimate numbers as a range

 1 Circle the range that describes each estimate.

a 30–40 40–50 50–60

I estimate that there are 42 cars in the car park.

b 20–30 30–40 40–50

There are about 28 children in my class.

c 50–60 60–70 70–80

I estimate that there are 75 pencils in that pot.

2 Estimate how many apples there are.

10–20   20–30   30–40   40–50

 1

a Estimate how many bananas there are. Give your answer as a range.

b Draw a ring around a group of 10 bananas, then keep making groups of 10 to help you count them.

c How many bananas are there altogether?

2

    a Estimate how many oranges there.
         Give your answer as a range.

    b Draw rings around groups of 10 oranges to help
         you count them.

    c How many oranges are there altogether?

3 Why is it easier to estimate a range than a number?

_____

_____

_____

Challenge 3 Without looking, write an estimate (as a range) for the number of
pages that are in an exercise book.

    a Estimate =

    b Count the first 10 pages in the exercise book and hold them
         between your fingers.

         Now you know what 10 pages look like, alter your range if
         you want to make it more accurate.

         New estimate =

    c Now count the pages to see what the actual answer is.

         There are   pages in total.

Unit 3 Whole numbers 3

Lesson 1: **Multiplying by 10 (2)**

Number (sidebar)

- Multiply 2-digit numbers by 10

 1

1 Kayla has written the answers to these multiplication questions, but some of her answers are wrong.

Put a ✓ or ✗ to show whether Kayla has answered correctly or not.

a 24 × 10 = 240 ☐   **b** 67 × 10 = 607 ☐

c 92 × 10 = 902 ☐   **d** 15 × 10 = 150 ☐

e 48 × 10 = 408 ☐   **f** 33 × 10 = 330 ☐

g 29 × 10 = 290 ☐   **h** 19 × 10 = 109 ☐

2 Copy each of the questions Kayla has got wrong and write the correct answer instead.

☐ ☐

☐ ☐

Challenge 2

1 Multiply each of the 2-digit numbers by 10. Write the number in the correct lanes.

H T U   H T U

a 52 × 10 = ☐☐☐   **b** 36 × 10 = ☐☐☐

c 44 × 10 = ☐☐☐   **d** 42 × 10 = ☐☐☐

e 91 × 10 = ☐☐☐   **f** 14 × 10 = ☐☐☐

g 74 × 10 = ☐☐☐   **h** 21 × 10 = ☐☐☐

2 Complete the sentences.

a 10 lots of 1 unit is   **b** 10 lots of 1 ten is

worth one ☐ .   worth one ☐ .

Your answers to these two questions are the reason why the digits shift a place when you make a number 10 times bigger.

34

3 Members of a swimming club are hoping to take part in a sponsored swim for charity. They each pay $10 to enter.

Complete the table to show how much money they will raise.

Number of swimmers	Total amount raised ($)
28	280
83	
	410
55	
12	
	890
69	
	620

Challenge 3

1 Without using numbers, describe what happens when you multiply a 2-digit number by 10.

_____

_____

_____

2 What do you think will happen to a 3-digit number when you multiply it by 10?

3 Write four examples of 3-digit calculations to explain your answer.

Number

Lesson 2: **Estimating and rounding**

* Estimate and round numbers

Challenge 1

Estimate how many kilometres each of the cars has travelled. Then write the distance to the nearest fuel station shown with a dot.

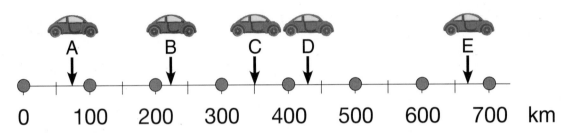

Car	Estimated distance travelled (km)	Distance to nearest fuel station (km)
A		
B		
C		
D		
E		

Challenge 2 1

a Estimate how many cars there are. Give your answer as a range.

Number

b Circle groups of 10 cars, to help you count them.

c How many cars are there altogether?

d Round this number to the nearest 10.

2

a Estimate how many motorbikes there are as a range.

b Circle groups of 10 motorbikes to help you count them.

c How many motorbikes are there altogether?

d Round this number to the nearest 10.

Challenge 3

1 Take two handfuls of small objects. Without counting, write an estimate of the number of objects. Give your answer as a range.

I estimate there are between [ ] and [ ].

2 Count out 10 of the objects so you can see what 10 look like. Alter your range if you want to make it more accurate.

My new estimate is between [ ] and [ ].

3 Now count the objects by sorting them into groups of 10.

There are [ ] objects in total.

4 Round the number of objects to the nearest 10.

Lesson 3: **Comparing numbers (2)**

- Use the > and < signs to compare 3-digit numbers

Challenge 1 Write the correct symbol (> or <) in the box between each pair of numbers.

a 56 ☐ 58   **b** 66 ☐ 73

c 12 ☐ 11   **d** 45 ☐ 49

e 18 ☐ 10   **f** 92 ☐ 98

g 23 ☐ 29   **h** 31 ☐ 32

Challenge 2

1 Write the correct symbol (> or <) in the box between each pair of numbers.

a 454 ☐ 445   **b** 127 ☐ 172   **c** 627 ☐ 276

d 841 ☐ 814   **e** 232 ☐ 223   **f** 303 ☐ 330

g 914 ☐ 941   **h** 893 ☐ 839   **i** 525 ☐ 535

2 Write a number that lies between each pair of numbers.

a 454, ☐ , 445   **b** 127, ☐ , 172   **c** 627, ☐ , 276

d 841, ☐ , 814   **e** 232, ☐ , 223   **f** 303, ☐ , 330

g 914, ☐ , 941   **h** 893, ☐ , 839   **i** 675, ☐ , 700

3 Rearrange the three digits in the given score, so that the HOME team wins every match.

Example:

HOME	VISITORS
1 4 2	1 2 4

a

HOME	VISITORS
5 9 3	☐ ☐ ☐

b

HOME	VISITORS
2 1 9	☐ ☐ ☐

c

HOME	VISITORS
1 8 3	☐ ☐ ☐

d

HOME	VISITORS
1 5 9	☐ ☐ ☐

e

HOME	VISITORS
2 5 4	☐ ☐ ☐

f

HOME	VISITORS
4 8 2	☐ ☐ ☐

 Challenge 3

1 Sam has compared pairs of 4-digit numbers. Some of his symbols are not correct. Put a ✓ or a ✗ to show whether the statement is right or wrong.

a 2895 > 2589 ☐   **b** 5673 < 5637 ☐

c 1409 < 1490 ☐   **d** 8049 > 4089 ☐

e 1123 > 1213 ☐   **f** 1752 < 1725 ☐

2 Write out each of Sam's incorrect answers again, but change the second number so that the comparison is true.

☐

Lesson 4: **Ordering numbers (2)**

Number

• Order 2- and 3-digit numbers

Challenge 1

These hotel room keys have been hung in the wrong order.
Order each set of numbers, smallest to largest.

a

| 28 | 85 | 82 | 58 | 52 |

b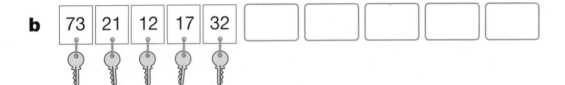

| 73 | 21 | 12 | 17 | 32 |

c

| 57 | 80 | 78 | 75 | 85 |

d

| 43 | 93 | 39 | 34 | 49 |

Challenge 2

1 Order each set of 3-digit hotel room numbers, smallest to largest.

a

| 238 | 819 | 283 | 198 | 231 |

b

| 464 | 446 | 404 | 644 | 646 |

c 518 185 158 351 315 ☐ ☐ ☐ ☐ ☐

d 387 724 713 703 317 ☐ ☐ ☐ ☐ ☐

e 425 452 432 428 429 ☐ ☐ ☐ ☐ ☐

2 All of these hotel room numbers begin with the digit 1.

Fill in the last 2 digits so that the rooms are in order, smallest to largest.

You can only use each digit once. Cross them out as you use them.

a 0 1 2 3 4 5 6 7 8 9

☐ 1 ☐ 1 ☐ 1 ☐ 1 ☐ 1 ☐

b Make different numbers in the same way, so the new hotel rooms are now in order, largest to smallest.

0 1 2 3 4 5 6 7 8 9

☐ 1 ☐ 1 ☐ 1 ☐ 1 ☐ 1 ☐

 Challenge 3

1 Use the digits 4, 1 and 7 to make six different 3-digit numbers. Write them in order, smallest to largest.

☐ ☐ ☐ ☐ ☐

2 Use the digits 9, 5 and 2 to make six different 3-digit numbers. Write them in order, largest to smallest.

☐ ☐ ☐ ☐ ☐

Number

Lesson 1: **Finding half**

• Find half of numbers up to 40

Challenge 1

1 The biscuits in each of these jars are shared between two people. How many does each person have?

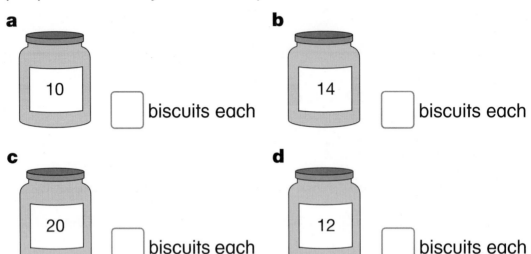

a

10

☐ biscuits each

b

14

☐ biscuits each

c

20

☐ biscuits each

d

12

☐ biscuits each

2 Match each number with the number that is half of it.

16 •

22 •

3 •

9 •

• $1\frac{1}{2}$

• 8

• $4\frac{1}{2}$

• 11

Challenge 2

1 The arrow points to half of the first number. 10 $\xrightarrow{\text{halved is}}$ 5

Complete these halving questions.

a 14 ⟶ ☐

b 17 ⟶ ☐

c 28 ⟶ ☐

d 25 ⟶ ☐

e ☐ ⟶ $5\frac{1}{2}$

f ☐ ⟶ 12

Number

2 Draw a line to match each number with its correct statement.

a 26 •

• Half of this number is $13\frac{1}{2}$.

b 19 •

• Half of this number ends in a 9.

c 27 •

• Half of this number is 13.

d 38 •

• Half of this number is just less than 10.

3 Write the halves for each of the numbers (from Question 2).

a 26 [ ]

b 19 [ ]

c 27 [ ]

d 38 [ ]

Challenge 3

Krishna has a jar of biscuits to share with a friend. She doesn't know how many are in the jar.

a Draw a circle around all the numbers that will end in a fraction when she halves them. For example, you will need to circle 15 because half of 15 is $7\frac{1}{2}$.

15 18 22 21 27 13 38 31 35 40 17 10 11 25

b Look carefully at the numbers. What do you notice?

_____

_____

_____

c Krishna shares out the biscuits and finds that she doesn't have to break any in half. What sort of a number was the total number of biscuits? _____

_____

☹ 😐 ☺

Number

Lesson 2: **Non-unitary fractions**

- Write fractions correctly
- Understand that fractions can show more than one part

You will need
- coloured pencils

 Colour each shape to show the fraction.

a $\frac{1}{2}$ b $\frac{3}{4}$ c $\frac{2}{4}$ d $\frac{2}{3}$ e $\frac{4}{5}$

Challenge 2

1 Write the fraction shown by each circle.

a 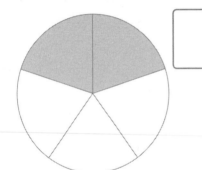   b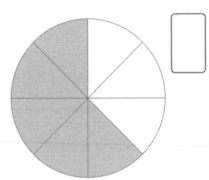

c 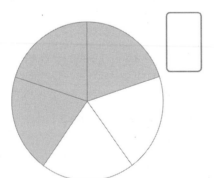   d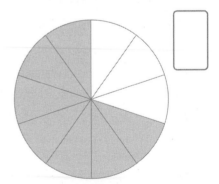

e 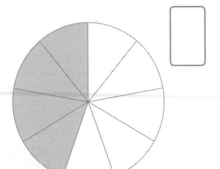   f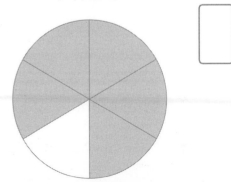

44

2 Ade cut some fruit into equal parts for his family to enjoy. Complete the table to show how much they ate.

Fruit	Number of equal parts altogether	Number of parts eaten	Fraction eaten
apple	4	2	$\frac{2}{4}$
melon	4	3	
pineapple	5	2	
orange	6	5	
pear			$\frac{2}{3}$
banana			$\frac{3}{5}$
watermelon			$\frac{4}{10}$

Challenge 3 Use these digits to write six different fractions. Complete the information about each one.

| 2 | 3 | 4 | 5 | 6 | 10 |

Example: 4 parts out of a total of 6 parts = $\frac{4}{6}$

a ☐ parts out of a total of ☐ parts = ☐

b ☐ parts out of a total of ☐ parts = ☐

c ☐ parts out of a total of ☐ parts = ☐

d ☐ parts out of a total of ☐ parts = ☐

e ☐ parts out of a total of ☐ parts = ☐

f ☐ parts out of a total of ☐ parts = ☐

Number

Number

Lesson 3: **Equivalent fractions**

You will need
• coloured pencils

• Recognise fractions that are worth the same

1 $\frac{2}{4}$ is the same as $\frac{1}{2}$. Colour $\frac{1}{2}$ of each of these shapes.

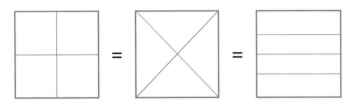

2 $\frac{4}{8}$ is also the same as $\frac{1}{2}$. Colour $\frac{4}{8}$ of each of these shapes.

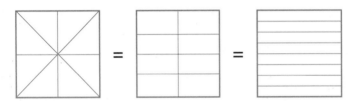

1 Colour the three remaining circles with the same amount as the first circle and write each new fraction in the box.

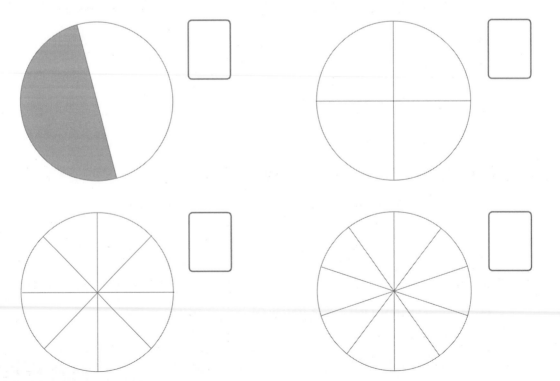

Number

2 4 friends buy pizzas that are all the same size.

Ali cuts a pizza into 2 equal slices and eats 1 of them.

Ben cuts a pizza into 10 equal slices.

Caila cuts a pizza into 4 equal slices.

Deepak cuts a pizza into 8 equal slices.

How many slices should each person eat so that they eat the same as Ali?

a Ben should eat ☐ slices.

b Caila should eat ☐ slices.

c Deepak should eat ☐ slices.

3 Circle the shapes that do **not** show $\frac{1}{2}$ shaded.

a

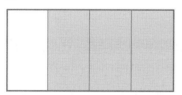

b

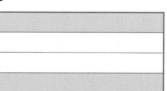

c

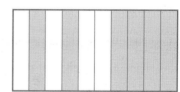

d

e

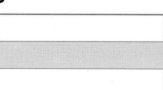

f

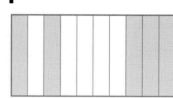

Challenge 3 Circle the fractions that are equal to $\frac{1}{2}$.

$\frac{3}{6}$ $\frac{2}{4}$ $\frac{50}{100}$ $\frac{6}{10}$ $\frac{4}{8}$ $\frac{5}{7}$ $\frac{6}{12}$ $\frac{8}{9}$ $\frac{10}{20}$

What do you notice about the numbers in fractions that equal $\frac{1}{2}$?

_____

_____

☹ 😐 ☺

Lesson 4: **Mixed fractions**

- Recognise simple mixed fractions

You will need
- coloured pencils
- ruler

Challenge 1

1 Colour $4\frac{1}{2}$ rectangles.

2 Colour $3\frac{1}{4}$ squares.

3 Colour $4\frac{3}{4}$ circles.

4 Colour $3\frac{1}{2}$ triangles.

Challenge 2

1 Kyle is painting coloured strips on a brick wall. He paints some whole bricks and then a fraction of the final brick.

Draw a line to match each strip with the correct mixed fraction.

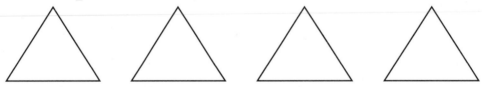

a — $2\frac{3}{4}$

b — $3\frac{1}{4}$

c — $3\frac{1}{2}$

d — $3\frac{1}{3}$

e — $2\frac{1}{2}$

f — $4\frac{1}{4}$

2 Complete the table to show more mixed fractions Kyle paints.

Number of whole bricks	Number of parts that the final brick is split into	Number of parts of the final brick Kyle paints	Total length of bricks as a mixed fraction
6	2	1	$6\frac{1}{2}$
4	4	1	
7	3	2	
5	2	1	
			$4\frac{3}{4}$
			$6\frac{3}{5}$
			$3\frac{8}{10}$

Challenge 3 Colour each of these amounts and then write the mixed fraction you have coloured.

a seven halves

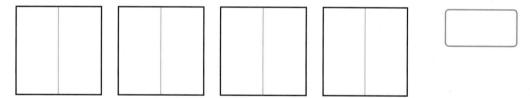

b eleven quarters

c eleven thirds

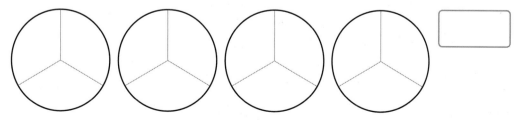

49

Lesson 5: **Ordering fractions**

• Order fractions or mixed fractions on a number line

Number (sidebar)

Challenge 1 Write the missing fractions.

a

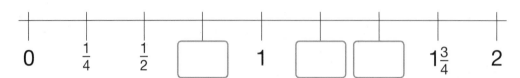

0   $\frac{1}{4}$ $\frac{1}{2}$ ☐   1   ☐   ☐ $1\frac{3}{4}$ 2

b

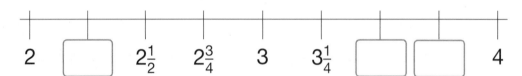

2   ☐ $2\frac{1}{2}$ $2\frac{3}{4}$ 3 $3\frac{1}{4}$ ☐   ☐   4

c

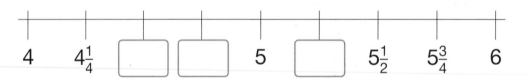

4   $4\frac{1}{4}$ ☐   ☐   5   ☐ $5\frac{1}{2}$ $5\frac{3}{4}$ 6

Challenge 2

1 Write the fractions shown on each number line.

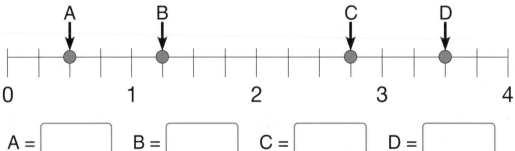

A = ☐   B = ☐   C = ☐   D = ☐

2

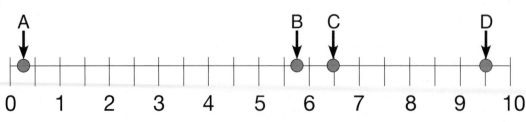

A = ☐   B = ☐   C = ☐   D = ☐

Number

3 Put these fractions in the correct order by labelling them on each number line.

a $4\frac{3}{4}$ $7\frac{3}{4}$ $\frac{1}{4}$ $6\frac{1}{2}$ $9\frac{1}{4}$ $3\frac{1}{2}$

b $8\frac{1}{4}$ $9\frac{3}{4}$ $\frac{3}{4}$ $2\frac{1}{2}$ $1\frac{1}{4}$ $5\frac{1}{2}$

c $6\frac{3}{4}$ $4\frac{1}{4}$ $1\frac{3}{4}$ $\frac{1}{2}$ $8\frac{3}{4}$ $3\frac{1}{2}$

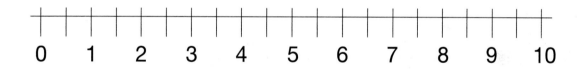

Challenge 3

1 Use the number line above to help you work out what number is halfway between:

a $\frac{1}{2}$ and 1

b 2 and 3

c $\frac{1}{4}$ and $\frac{3}{4}$

d $3\frac{1}{2}$ and 4

2 Amir thinks of a mixed fraction. It is more than 1, less than 3 and ends with $\frac{1}{2}$. What could it be?

51

Number

Lesson 6: **Fractions and division**

- Understand how finding fractions is linked to division

Challenge 1 Draw a line to match each fraction with the division calculation.

$\frac{1}{4}$ of 12 •   • 12 ÷ 3

$\frac{1}{8}$ of 80 •   • 12 ÷ 2

$\frac{1}{2}$ of 80 •   • 80 ÷ 8

$\frac{1}{2}$ of 36 •   • 20 ÷ 4

$\frac{1}{3}$ of 12 •   • 80 ÷ 10

$\frac{1}{5}$ of 20 •   • 12 ÷ 4

$\frac{1}{10}$ of 80 •   • 36 ÷ 2

$\frac{1}{4}$ of 20 •   • 80 ÷ 2

$\frac{1}{2}$ of 12 •   • 20 ÷ 5

Challenge 2 **1** Myesha has different piles of rice grains. She needs to find fractions of these amounts. Fill in the table to show the division calculations she should use to work out the answers.

Number of rice piles	Fraction needed	Division	Answer
20	$\frac{1}{2}$	20 ÷ 2	10
16	$\frac{1}{2}$		
24	$\frac{1}{4}$		
35	$\frac{1}{5}$		
30	$\frac{1}{10}$		
18	$\frac{1}{2}$		
12	$\frac{1}{4}$		
26	$\frac{1}{2}$		

Number

2 Work backwards from the division calculations to write the fraction questions they are based on. You do not need to work out the answers.

Example: $32 \div 2 = \frac{1}{2}$ of 32

a $20 \div 4 =$ [ ]

b $14 \div 2 =$ [ ]

c $15 \div 5 =$ [ ]

d $24 \div 6 =$ [ ]

e $30 \div 3 =$ [ ]

f $32 \div 2 =$ [ ]

g $25 \div 5 =$ [ ]

h $18 \div 2 =$ [ ]

Challenge 3 Use the fraction and number cards to make questions. Then write each of them as a division and work out the answer.

$\frac{1}{10}$ of $\frac{1}{2}$ of $\frac{1}{5}$ of $\frac{1}{4}$ of

40   20   80

Example: $\frac{1}{5}$ of 80 = 80 ÷ 5 = 16

Can you make the same number in two different ways? How?

Lesson 7: **Finding fractions of shapes**

- Find halves, thirds, quarters and tenths of shapes

Number

1 Colour each shape to show the fraction.

a  Show $\frac{2}{3}$ **b** 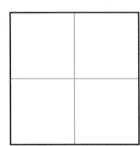 Show $\frac{1}{4}$

c  Show $\frac{2}{4}$ **d** 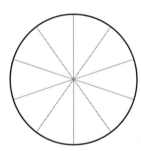 Show $\frac{5}{10}$

e 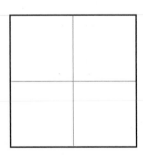 Show $\frac{3}{4}$ **f** 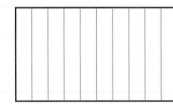 Show $\frac{7}{10}$

2 Two of the fractions you have coloured in Question 1 are equal to $\frac{1}{2}$. Which are they?

[ ] and [ ]

1 What fraction of each shape is shaded?

a  **b** 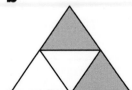 **c**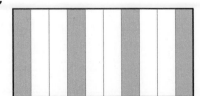

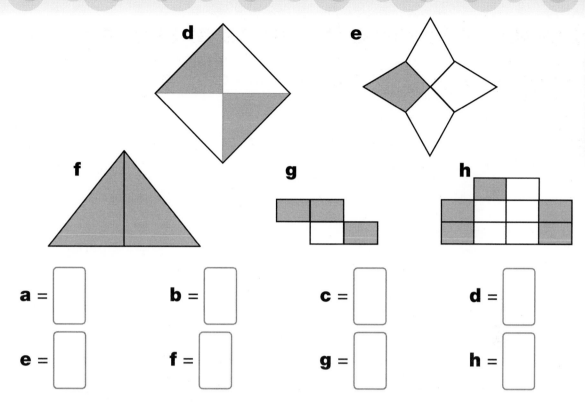

a = [ ]   b = [ ]   c = [ ]   d = [ ]

e = [ ]   f = [ ]   g = [ ]   h = [ ]

2 Which of the shapes in Question 1 have half shaded?
Write the letters below.

_____

Challenge 3 A rectangle is split into an even number of equal parts.

How many parts would you have to shade so that half is shaded?

There are many answers to this question.

    a Use these blank rectangles to show your answers.

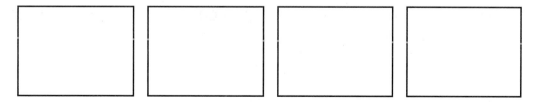

    b The fractions I have shaded are [ ] , [ ] , [ ]

and [ ] .

Lesson 8: **Finding fractions of numbers**

• Find halves, thirds, quarters and tenths of numbers

Challenge 1 Draw a ring around half of each pile.

a

$\frac{1}{2}$ of 20 is [ ]

b

$\frac{1}{2}$ of 12 is [ ]

c

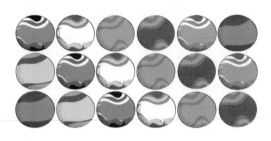

$\frac{1}{2}$ of 18 is [ ]

d

$\frac{1}{2}$ of 22 is [ ]

Challenge 2

1 A clothing shop is having a sale. What are the new prices?

a $\frac{1}{2}$ of $18 = $ [ ]

b $\frac{1}{10}$ of $50 = $ [ ]

c $\frac{1}{4}$ of $12 = $ [ ]

d $\frac{1}{4}$ of $40 = $ [ ]

e $\frac{1}{10}$ of $30 = $ [ ]

f $\frac{1}{4}$ of $8 = $ [ ]

g $\frac{1}{3}$ of $15 = $ [ ]

h $\frac{1}{2}$ of $26 = $ [ ]

2 Noah is in a shop where the price of everything is reduced. He works out some prices, but he has got some of them wrong.

Tick (✓) Noah's calculations if you think he has got them right. Cross (✗) any that he has got wrong.

a $\frac{1}{3}$ of \$12 = \$6 ☐   **b** $\frac{1}{4}$ of \$36 = \$9 ☐   **c** $\frac{1}{2}$ of \$18 = \$9 ☐

d $\frac{1}{3}$ of \$21 = \$7 ☐   **e** $\frac{1}{2}$ of \$14 = \$8 ☐   **f** $\frac{1}{2}$ of \$34 = \$19 ☐

3 For each of Noah's wrong calculations, write the correct answer.

☐

 Challenge 3

1 a Write two fractions of number calculations that have the answer 10.

Example: $\frac{1}{4}$ of 40 = 10 $\frac{1}{8}$ of 80 = 10

☐ ☐

b Write two fractions of number calculations that have the answer 7.

☐ ☐

c Write two fractions of number calculations that have the answer 13.

☐ ☐

2 a Can you find two fractions of number calculations that have the answer $4\frac{1}{2}$?

☐ ☐

b Can you find two fractions of number calculations that have the answer $9\frac{1}{2}$?

☐ ☐

57

Lesson 1: **Addition and subtraction facts to 20**

* Know addition and subtraction facts for numbers to 20

 1 Draw a line to match each question to its answer.

6 + 5 •   • 9

10 – 3 •   • 12

2 + 7 •   • 11

10 – 5 •   • 7

8 + 4 •   • 6

12 – 6 •   • 5

2 a Add 4 apples to the number you can see.

How many are there now? _____

b Take away 9 apples from the number you can see.

How many are there now? _____

 1 Complete these calculations.

a 5 + 14 = _____   **b** 13 + 2 = _____

c 20 – 8 = _____   **d** 19 – 12 = _____

e 15 + 4 = _____   **f** 12 + 6 = _____

g 11 – 9 = _____   **h** 11 + 3 = _____

2 Use the numbers in each image to write one addition and one subtraction calculation.

a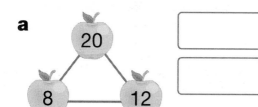

b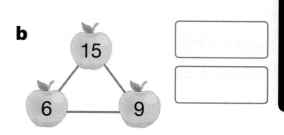

c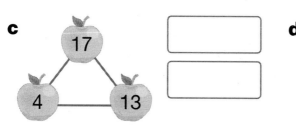

d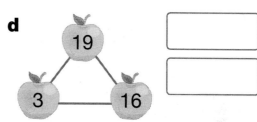

3 a What is 18 plus 2?

b What is 5 less than 12?

c What is the difference between 14 and 19?

d What is 8 more than 9?

e What is the total of 4 and 14?

 1 Write two additions and two subtractions that give the answer 16.

2 Write two additions and two subtractions that give the answer 12.

Number

Number

Lesson 2: **Multiples of 100 that total 1000**

- Identify multiples of 100 with a total of 1000

You will need
- coloured pencils

Challenge 1

Multiples of 100 that make 1000 are similar to pairs that make 10. Complete these pairs that make 10.

a $4 + \boxed{} = 10$

b $3 + \boxed{} = 10$

c $\boxed{} + 8 = 10$

d $\boxed{} + 5 = 10$

e $\boxed{} + 2 = 10$

f $7 + \boxed{} = 10$

g $6 + \boxed{} = 10$

h $9 + \boxed{} = 10$

Challenge 2

1 a Colour pairs of balloons in the same colour to show the multiples of 100 that make 1000.

100 200 300 400 500 500 600 700 800 900

b What do you notice about the pairs?

_____

_____

2 Write the missing multiples.

a $600 + \boxed{} = 1000$

b $900 + \boxed{} = 1000$

c $\boxed{} + 500 = 1000$

d $300 + \boxed{} = 1000$

e $\boxed{} + 200 = 1000$

f $100 + \boxed{} = 1000$

g $400 + \boxed{} = 1000$

h $\boxed{} + 800 = 1000$

3 Look at the pairs in Question 2 and compare them with pairs that you know that make 10. What do you notice?

_____

_____

_____

Challenge 3 Mia has a set of balloons with multiples of 100 on them.

She puts the balloons into three different pairs that total 1000.

Look at each clue to work out the pairs and write them on the balloons.

a In the first pair, one of her balloons is 200 less than the other one.

What are the numbers on Mia's balloons?

b In the second pair, one of her balloons has the largest number on it.

What are the numbers on Mia's balloons?

c In the third pair, both of the numbers begin with digits that are odd.

What are the numbers on Mia's balloons?

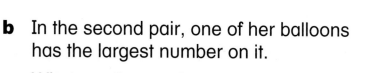

Number

Lesson 3: **Multiples of 5 that total 100**

• Identify multiples of 5 with a total of 100

 Challenge 1

1 Colour all of the multiples of 5.

(40) (23) (81) (60) (38) (57) (25)

(29) (75) (39) (20) (41) (80) (94)

2 Some of the numbers you have coloured add together to make 100. Draw lines to match up pairs with a total of 100.

 Challenge 2

1 Each section of a stick is worth 5. The total value of all the sections is 100.

Look at each stick and write the pair of multiples of 5 that it shows.

a

35 + [   ] = 100

b

75 + [   ] = 100

c

10 + [   ] = 100

d

50 + [   ] = 100

Number

2 Shade each stick in two colours to show different pairs of
multiples of 5 that make 100.

a

[ ] + [ ] = 100

b

[ ] + [ ] = 100

c

[ ] + [ ] = 100

d

[ ] + [ ] = 100

e

[ ] + [ ] = 100

Challenge 3

1 How many different
pairs of multiples of
5 can you find with
a total of 100? Write
them down.

2 How did you work out
the answers?

_____

_____

_____

Number

Lesson 4: **Adding and subtracting 10 and multiples of 10**

• Add and subtract multiples of 10 to and from numbers up to 1000

Challenge 1

1 Look carefully at each number line. Write the calculation it shows.

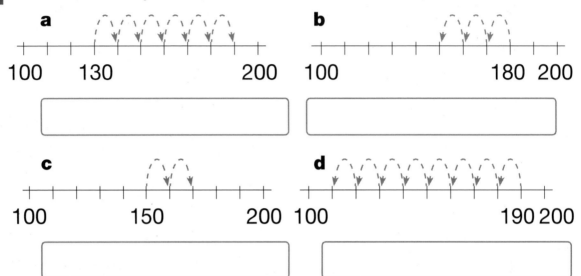

a

100   130   200

b

100   180 200

c

100   150   200

d

100   190 200

2 Answer these:

a $46 + 50 = \boxed{}$

b $75 - 30 = \boxed{}$

c $92 - 60 = \boxed{}$

d $34 + 80 = \boxed{}$

Challenge 2

1 Six children are playing a computer game. Some of them have gained extra points, but some of them have lost points.

a Complete the table to show each child's new score.

Name	Score	Change in points	New score
Sophie	582	60 less	
Hassan	629	30 more	
Jack	710	20 less	
Lucas	361	50 less	
Krishna	815	70 more	
Kian	125	90 more	

b Which children's scores had a hundreds digit that changed as well as the tens digit? _____ and _____.

2 Complete these calculations.

a 285 + [ ] = 345

b 774 + 40 = [ ]

c 128 − [ ] = 108

d 456 + [ ] = 496

e [ ] − 30 = 639

f 225 − 50 = [ ]

 3 Write each calculation and work out the answer.

a Erin is running a 400-metre race. She has 80 metres to run before reaching the finish line. How far has she run already?

b There are 387 birds in a field. Another 30 birds fly in. How many birds are there now altogether?

c Alicia has saved $527. She spends $40. How much does she have left?

d William has 141 points in a computer game. He scores an extra 50 bonus points. What is his new score?

Lesson 5: **Adding 100 and multiples of 100**

- Add multiples of 100 to numbers up to 1000

You will need
- coloured pencils

 1 Draw a line to match each calculation with the correct answer.

250 + 100 •   • 970

340 + 100 •   • 350

870 + 100 •   • 440

420 + 100 •   • 520

2 Look carefully at these calculations. In each answer, colour the digit that has changed.

a 286 + 300 = | 5 | 8 | 6 |

b 338 + 400 = | 7 | 3 | 8 |

c 466 + 500 = | 9 | 6 | 6 |

d 299 + 600 = | 8 | 9 | 9 |

 1

| 100 | 300 | 500 | 600 | 200 | 400 | 50 |

| 80 | 30 | 90 | 8 | 2 | 1 | 6 |

Use these place value cards to make eight questions in which you add a multiple of 100 to a 3-digit number. Work out each answer.

For example: 531 + 300 = 831

a ☐ + ☐ = ☐   **b** ☐ + ☐ = ☐

c ☐ + ☐ = ☐   **d** ☐ + ☐ = ☐

e ☐ + ☐ = ☐   **f** ☐ + ☐ = ☐

g ☐ + ☐ = ☐   **h** ☐ + ☐ = ☐

2 What do you add to get from the first number to the second?

a From 429 to 929 ☐   **b** From 105 to 905 ☐

c From 728 to 828 ☐   **d** From 361 to 661 ☐

e From 233 to 833 ☐   **f** From 517 to 917 ☐

3 What do you notice about all your answers in Question 2?

_____

Challenge 3

[+ 400]   [+ 500]   [+ 600]   [+ 700]

Ruby has four addition cards. Use these to write your own calculations to fit the following clues.

a A calculation with the answer 752.

☐

b A calculation in which the answer has a 9 in the hundreds place.

☐

c A calculation to which the answer is 483.

☐

d A calculation in which all the hundreds digits are even.

☐

e A calculation with a 4-digit answer.

☐

☹ 😐 ☺

Lesson 6: **Adding three or more small numbers**

• Add three or more small numbers together

Challenge 1 Work out these addition calculations.

a 2 + ☐ = 7

b 1 + 7 = ☐

c 3 + ☐ = 9

d ☐ + 5 = 8

e 1 + 3 + ☐ = 6

f 4 + 2 + 3 = ☐

g 5 + ☐ + 2 = 11

h 6 + 3 + ☐ = 16

Challenge 2 **1** Ella takes three digit cards at a time and adds them together. She makes different totals.

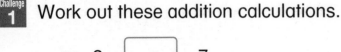

| 2 | 4 | 3 | 7 | 8 | 9 | 1 |

Which digits does she use to make these totals?

a 19 = ☐ + ☐ + ☐

b 18 = ☐ + ☐ + ☐

c 14 = ☐ + ☐ + ☐

d 17 = ☐ + ☐ + ☐

e 20 = ☐ + ☐ + ☐

f 13 = ☐ + ☐ + ☐

Number

2 Circle the two numbers you would add first in each calculation and then work out the answer.

a 5 + 7 + 4 + 3 = ☐

b 6 + 8 + 3 = ☐

c 9 + 2 + 4 + 2 = ☐

d 5 + 3 + 8 + 2 = ☐

e 9 + 4 + 2 + 3 = ☐

f 9 + 4 + 6 + 6 = ☐

g 5 + 3 + 7 + 1 = ☐

h 1 + 6 + 9 + 6 = ☐

 Challenge 3

1 Alicia spins a spinner and gets these numbers:

4 3 8 7

How many different totals can she make by adding three numbers at a time?

Write all the different calculations possible.

2 Alicia spins the spinner again and gets the number 9. She uses this as well as her first four numbers.

Make five different totals by adding four numbers at a time.

Write each of the different calculations.

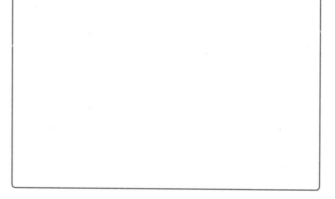

69

Lesson 7: **Using the = sign to represent equality**

- Understand what the = sign means
- Use the = sign to represent equality

Challenge 1
Each answer box should contain a different digit, from 0 to 9.

Choose a digit for each answer box so that the statements are correct.

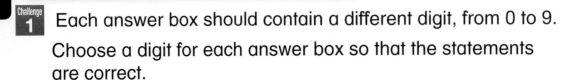

| 0 | 1 | 2 | 3 | 4 | 5 | 6 | 7 | 8 | 9 |

a ☐ + 8 = 10

b 3 + ☐ = 11

c ☐ − 5 = 2

d 7 − ☐ = 3 + 3

e 9 + ☐ = 12

f 9 − ☐ = 2 + 3

g ☐ − 4 = 9 − 8

h 8 + 8 = 10 + ☐

Challenge 2

1 Each of these see-saws is balanced. Write a statement in the second box that has an answer that is equal to the statement in the first box.

a Write a subtraction.

b Write a subtraction.

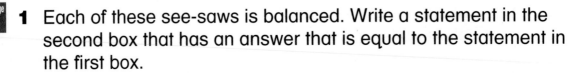

| 14 + 5 | = | ☐ |

| 15 − 9 | = | ☐ |

c Write an addition.

d Write an addition.

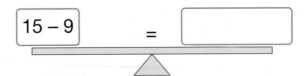

| 18 − 6 | = | ☐ |

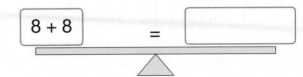

| 8 + 8 | = | ☐ |

Number

2 Now write two pairs of statements of your own. One side of each see-saw should be an addition and the other side a subtraction.

a

=

b

=

3 Not all of these statements are true. Write true or false next to each one.

a $8 + 9 = 20 - 3$ _____

b $3 + 13 = 8 + 10$ _____

c $16 - 7 = 4 + 4$ _____

d $4 + 7 = 5 + 6$ _____

e $17 - 7 = 19 - 5$ _____

f $12 - 4 = 7 + 1$ _____

Challenge 3

1 On one side of an equals sign is the number 12.

Write as many statements as you can to give the answer 12.

2 On one side of an equals sign is $4 + 9$.

Write as many subtraction statements as you can on the other side.

Lesson 8: **Addition in any order**

- Change the order of an addition to solve it

Challenge 1

For each calculation, work out the answer then check your answer by writing the numbers in a different order.

For example: 5 + 2 + 3 = 10

Check: 3 + 2 + 5 = 10

a 7 + 2 + 3 = ☐

Check: ☐

b 4 + 2 + 9 = ☐

Check: ☐

c 1 + 6 + 2 = ☐

Check: ☐

d 7 + 3 + 6 = ☐

Check: ☐

Challenge 2

1 These two strips have been split into three sections to show totals of 30. They show how numbers can be added in a different order to get the same answer.

3	20	7
20	7	3

a Do the same for strips equal to 20.

b Do the same for strips equal to 28.

Number

2 For each question, choose any three of these numbers and add them together. Then add them in a different order to check you are correct.

| 21 14 5 15 9 7 12 4 25 |

For example:

14 + 5 + 7

14 + 5 = 19   19 + 7 = 26

5 + 7 = 12   12 + 14 = 26

a ☐ + ☐ = ☐   ☐ + ☐ = ☐

b ☐ + ☐ = ☐   ☐ + ☐ = ☐

c ☐ + ☐ = ☐   ☐ + ☐ = ☐

d ☐ + ☐ = ☐   ☐ + ☐ = ☐

3 Jasmine adds three numbers together.

She adds the first two numbers and makes 20.

When she adds the third number. The total is odd.

a What could Jasmine's numbers be? ☐

b Show how you could add Jasmine's numbers in a different order to get the same total.

Number

Lesson 1: **Totals of multiples of 5 and 100 (1)**

- Recognise multiples of 5 with a total of 100 and multiples of 100 with a total of 1000

You will need
- coloured pencils

Challenge 1

Each grid contains 100 small squares.

Look in this box to find pairs of numbers that make 100 and use two different colours to show your calculation on each grid.

5	10	15	20	25
30	35	40	45	50
55	60	65	70	75
	80	85	90	95

For example:

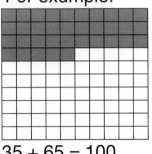

35 + 65 = 100

a

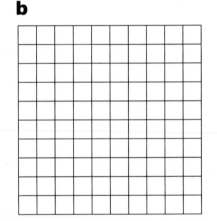

[ ] + [ ] = 100

b

[ ] + [ ] = 100

c

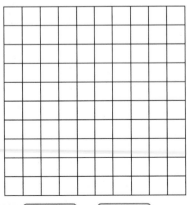

[ ] + [ ] = 100

d

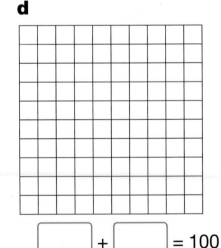

[ ] + [ ] = 100

Number

Challenge 2

1 Complete these calculations.

a $65 + \boxed{} = 100$

b $\boxed{} + 700 = 1000$

c $\boxed{} + 80 = 100$

d $100 + \boxed{} = 1000$

e $1000 - \boxed{} = 800$

f $45 + \boxed{} = 100$

2 a There are 1000 seats in a stadium. 700 of them have people sitting in them.

How many are empty? seats

b Isaac has \$65. How much more does he need to save to buy a \$100 train ticket? \$  more

c A plane is going on a 1000 km journey. It has already travelled 200 km. How much further does it have to go? km

Challenge 3

1 Each of these calculations contains three different numbers. Each number is a multiple of 5. Write the numbers in the boxes.

a $40 + \boxed{} + \boxed{} = 100$

b $50 + \boxed{} + \boxed{} = 100$

c $100 - \boxed{} - \boxed{} = 20$

d $100 - 10 - \boxed{} = \boxed{}$

2 How many different calculations can you find where three multiples of 100 add together to make 1000?

For example: $600 + 200 + 200 = 1000$ $\boxed{}$

☹ 😐 ☺

Lesson 2: **Adding pairs of 2-digit numbers (1)**

• Add a pair of 2-digit numbers

 1 Show how you would partition these 2-digit numbers.

Example:

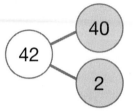

a

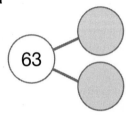

b

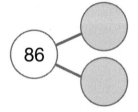

c

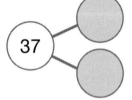

2 Complete each calculation.

a 12 + 14 = ☐

b 14 + 15 = ☐

c 13 + 15 = ☐

d 12 + 13 = ☐

1 Use the number lines to show your working for each calculation.

a 68 + 22 = ☐

68

b 38 + 52 = ☐

52

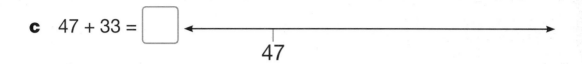

c 47 + 33 = ☐

47

d 21 + 78 = ☐

78

2 Use these digit cards to make 2-digit additions.

    | 2 | 5 | 6 | 3 | 8 |

Show your working in the large boxes.

a What is the smallest total you can make with these digits?

☐☐ + ☐☐ = ☐

b What is the largest total you can make with these digits?

☐☐ + ☐☐ = ☐

Challenge 3

1 Circle the pair of numbers that add to 64.

36 + 19   35 + 29   42 + 13

2 Circle the pair of numbers with a total that is closest to 100.

73 + 39   88 + 27   54 + 48

☹ 😐 ☺

Number

Lesson 3: **Subtracting pairs of 2-digit numbers (1)**

• Subtract a pair of 2-digit numbers

Challenge 1

Jamie subtracts a pair of 2-digit numbers and uses a number line to show his working. He counts back in 10s and 1s each time.

Look carefully at his sketches and calculate each answer.

a 38 – 12 = ☐

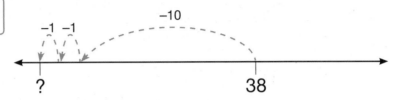

b 49 – 13 = ☐

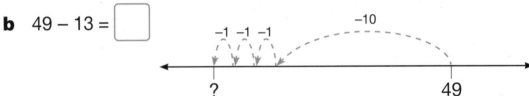

c 68 – 17 = ☐

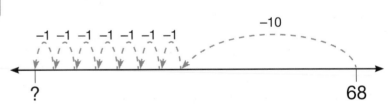

d 53 – 11 = ☐

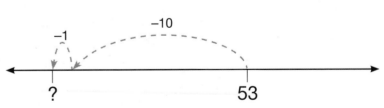

Challenge 2

1 Use the number line to show your working for each calculation.

a 73 – 19 = ☐

b 52 – 38 = ☐

c $77 - 28 =$ ☐ ⟵————————————————⟶

d $92 - 33 =$ ☐ ⟵————————————————⟶

e $63 - 38 =$ ☐ ⟵————————————————⟶

2 Use these digit cards to make 2-digit subtractions.

| 1 | 5 | 4 | 9 | 3 |

Show your working in the large boxes.

a What is the smallest answer you can make with these digits?

☐☐ – ☐☐ = ☐

b What is the largest answer you can make with these digits?

☐☐ – ☐☐ = ☐

Challenge 3 Show your working in the large boxes.

a Anaya thinks of a number. She subtracts 45 from it and ends up with 41. What was the number she thought of?

b Anaya thinks of another number. This time she adds 29 to it and ends up with 92.

What was the number she thought of?

Number

Lesson 4: **Adding 3-digit and 2-digit numbers (1)**

• Add 3-digit and 2-digit numbers together

Challenge 1

Partition the numbers, then use the number line to help you find the total.

Example:

| 4 | 1 | 8 | + | 2 | 5 |

| 4 | 1 | 8 | + | 2 | 0 | + | 5 | = | 443 |

a

| 2 | 1 | 5 | + | 3 | 2 |

[ ] + [ ] = [ ]

⟷

b

| 3 | 0 | 8 | + | 5 | 1 |

[ ] + [ ] = [ ]

⟷

c

| 2 | 4 | 7 | + | 2 | 2 |

[ ] + [ ] = [ ]

⟷

d

| 4 | 2 | 0 | + | 7 | 9 |

[ ] + [ ] = [ ]

⟷

Challenge 2

1 Take one number from the top set and one from the bottom set to answer the questions. Use the number lines to work out and show your answer.

| 372 | 411 | 833 | 625 | 761 | 201 | 670 | 105 | 155 |

| 89 | 82 | 47 | 46 | 36 | 77 | 39 | 59 | 63 |

a What is the largest total you can make?

☐ + ☐ = ⟵——————————→

b What is the smallest total you can make?

☐ + ☐ = ⟵——————————→

2 Write three more additions.

a ☐ + ☐ =

⟵——————————————————→

b ☐ + ☐ =

⟵——————————————————→

c ☐ + ☐ =

⟵——————————————————→

Challenge 3 Write each calculation and work out the answer.

a Mia is on page 146 of her book. She has 57 pages to go. How many pages does the book have altogether?

b What is the sum of 428 and 85?

Number

Lesson 5: **Adding a single-digit number to a 3-digit number**

• Add single-digit numbers to 3-digit numbers

You will need
• coloured pencil

Challenge 1

Look carefully at these calculations.
Colour the digit in each answer that has changed.

a | 4 | 2 | 4 | + | 3 | = | 4 | 2 | 7 |

b | 3 | 5 | 5 | + | 4 | = | 3 | 5 | 9 |

c | 2 | 7 | 7 | + | 2 | = | 2 | 7 | 9 |

d | 1 | 5 | 3 | + | 5 | = | 1 | 5 | 8 |

e | 2 | 5 | 4 | + | 3 | = | 2 | 5 | 7 |

f | 3 | 7 | 0 | + | 9 | = | 3 | 7 | 9 |

Challenge 2

1 Luisa adds a single-digit number to each 3-digit number so that the tens digit as well as the units digit changes. Write down the additions.

For example: | 3 | 2 | 7 | $327 + 5 = 332$

H   T   U

a | 4 | 0 | 3 |

H   T   U

b | 7 | 3 | 4 |

H   T   U

$\boxed{} + \boxed{} = \boxed{}$

c | 2 | 7 | 8 |

H   T   U

d | 3 | 8 | 6 |

H   T   U

$\boxed{} + \boxed{} = \boxed{}$

82

2 What do you add to get from the first number to the second?

a From 472 to 478 ☐ **b** From 237 to 246 ☐

c From 892 to 900 ☐ **d** From 555 to 562 ☐

3 Add 9 to each of these numbers.

Example: 573 → 582

a 263 → ☐ **b** 224 → ☐ **c** 884 → ☐

Challenge 3 Write addition calculations to match the clues. For each one add 6, 7, 8 or 9 to 3-digit numbers.

a An addition where the answer is odd

☐

b An addition to which the answer is larger than 685

☐

c An addition with the answer 304

☐

d An addition where the hundreds, tens and ones digits all change

☐

☹ 😐 ☺

Number

Lesson 6: **Subtracting a single-digit number from a 3-digit number**

* Subtract single-digit numbers from 3-digit numbers

1 Use the number line to help you subtract these numbers.

438 439 440 441 442 443 444 445 446 447 448 449 450 451 452

a 440 − 2 = ☐   **b** 450 − 6 = ☐

c 447 − 7 = ☐   **d** 452 − 9 = ☐

e 452 − 3 = ☐   **f** 450 − 5 = ☐

2 Cover up the number line.

Work out each subtraction in your head. When you have finished, uncover the number line to check your answers.

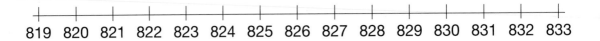

819 820 821 822 823 824 825 826 827 828 829 830 831 832 833

a 832 − 4 = ☐   **b** 825 − 4 = ☐

c 829 − 8 = ☐   **d** 828 − 5 = ☐

e 830 − 7 = ☐   **f** 825 − 3 = ☐

g 831 − 9 = ☐   **h** 830 − 6 = ☐

i 831 − 5 = ☐

Number

Challenge 2

1 Use subtraction to work backwards and calculate the missing numbers in these addition questions.

For example:

? + 4 = 148   148 − 4 = 144   So, 144 + 4 = 148

a   ? + 8 = 249

[ ] − [ ] = [ ]

So, [ ] + 8 = 249

b   ? + 3 = 502

[ ] − [ ] = [ ]

So, [ ] + 3 = 502

c   ? + 7 = 450

[ ] − [ ] = [ ]

So, [ ] + 7 = 450

d   ? + 8 = 803

[ ] − [ ] = [ ]

So, [ ] + 8 = 803

2 What do you subtract to get from the first number to the second?

a From 258 to 252 [ ]

b From 531 to 526 [ ]

c From 148 to 139 [ ]

d From 682 to 675 [ ]

Challenge 3

| 9 | 0 | 5 | 6 |

Use the digit cards to make five different calculations in which you subtract a single-digit number from a 3-digit number.

Write your subtractions and work out the answers.

85

Number

Lesson 7: **Adding multiples of 10 and 100 to 3-digit numbers**

- Find 20, 30, ..., 90, 100, 200, 300 more than a 3-digit number

You will need
- coloured pencil

 1 Colour the multiples of 10. If a number is not a multiple of 10, leave it blank.

| 50 | 20 | 42 | 78 | 200 | 60 | 40 | 300 |

| 100 | 62 | 156 | 30 | 88 | 39 | 70 | 29 |

2 Use the number line to help you find the total of these numbers.

300 310 320 330 340 350 360 370 380 390 400 410 420

a 320 + 20 = ☐   **b** 330 + 30 = ☐

c 300 + 90 = ☐   **d** 380 + 40 = ☐

 1 Join each box on the top with any of the boxes on the bottom.

| 419 g | 551 g | 204 g | 150 g | 925 g | 844 g |

| 20 g | 300 g | 50 g | 90 g | 200 g | 40 g |

Work out the total weight of the boxes you have matched up.

a ☐ + ☐ = ☐   **b** ☐ + ☐ = ☐

c ☐ + ☐ = ☐   **d** ☐ + ☐ = ☐

e ☐ + ☐ = ☐   **f** ☐ + ☐ = ☐

Number

2 Use the large box to draw your answer or sketch a number line to help.

A bus has travelled 142 km of its journey. It has to drive 50 km more to the coast and then another 30 km to its destination.

How far does the bus travel altogether?

1 Circle true or false next to each statement.

a 362 + 40 = 202 + 200   true / false

b 529 + 90 = 589 + 40   true / false

c 277 + 20 = 267 + 50   true / false

d 636 + 50 = 646 + 20   true / false

e 402 + 30 = 132 + 200   true / false

f 480 + 100 = 530 + 50   true / false

2 For each of your false answers in Question 1, change the last number to make the statement true.

Lesson 8: **Subtract multiples of 10 and 100 from 3-digit numbers**

• Find 20, 30, ... 90, 100, 200, 300 less than 3-digit numbers

Challenge 1 Use the number line to help you subtract the numbers.

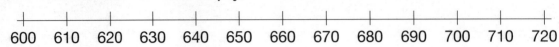

a   680 − 50 = [ ]　　　b   670 − 30 = [ ]

c   700 − 80 = [ ]　　　d   720 − 20 = [ ]

e   710 − 40 = [ ]　　　f   660 − 30 = [ ]

Challenge 2

1 Write six new subtractions. You have the starting number. Choose a multiple of 10 to subtract, then work out the answer.

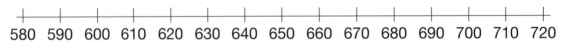

a   670 − [ ] = [ ]　　　b   710 − [ ] = [ ]

c   700 − [ ] = [ ]　　　d   720 − [ ] = [ ]

e   680 − [ ] = [ ]　　　f   690 − [ ] = [ ]

2 Some friends go into a shop and spend some of their savings. The numbers show how much money they had before shopping and how much they spent.

How much does each person have left when they leave the shop?

Name	Savings before shopping		Amount spent		
Azim	$125	−	$30	=	[ ]
Ben	$452	−	$200	=	[ ]
Clara	$378	−	$80	=	[ ]

Name	Savings before shopping		Amount spent		
Dion	$277	–	$60	=	
Ella	$302	–	$100	=	
Fatima	$528	–	$300	=	
Georgia	$450	–	$90	=	
Imani	$139	–	$70	=	
Joe	$184	–	$20	=	
Krishna	$266	–	$40	=	

Challenge 3

Abdul thinks he has found a method for subtracting multiples of 10 from 3-digit numbers. He writes three steps:

Step 1: Cross off the final digit from both the 3-digit number and the multiple of 10. For example, 156 – 70 becomes 15 – 7

Step 2: Work out the answer to the subtraction.   15 – 7 = 8

Step 3: Write the digit that you crossed off from the 3-digit number on the end again.   86

Try three different calculations to test Abdul's idea:

Number

Lesson 1: **Totals of multiples of 5 and 100 (2)**

- Recall multiples of 5 with a total of 100 and multiples of 100 with a total of 1000

The sum of each pair of numbers is 100. Choose the correct number from the cards to go in each box.

| 30 | 70 | 20 | 10 | 40 | 90 | 50 | 60 | 80 |

a 10 + ☐   **b** 20 + ☐   **c** 30 + ☐

d 40 + ☐   **e** 50 + ☐   **f** 60 + ☐

g 70 + ☐   **h** 80 + ☐   **i** 90 + ☐

1 Asma writes these pairs of multiples of 5. Put a tick (✓) in the box if the pair equals 100 or a cross (✗) if it does not.

a 25 + 85 ☐   **b** 60 + 40 ☐   **c** 5 + 90 ☐

d 10 + 80 ☐   **e** 45 + 65 ☐   **f** 15 + 85 ☐

g 75 + 35 ☐   **h** 90 + 20 ☐   **i** 75 + 15 ☐

2 For each pair in Question 1 that does not equal 100, write the correct pairs here. The first one has been done for you.

25 + 85 could be 25 + 75 or 85 + 15

Number

3 Each number in this grid is a multiple of 5. Each row adds up to 100. Fill in the missing numbers.

65	
	80
5	
25	
	90
85	
45	
	40
70	

4 Each number in this grid is a multiple of 100. Each row adds up to 1000. Fill in the missing numbers.

800	
	500
100	
400	
	700
200	
900	
	300
600	

Challenge 3

1 Arun writes 60 + 40 = 100 and then notices that if he adds a zero on the end of each of the numbers, the calculation becomes equal to 1000. 600 + 400 = 1000.

How many similar pairs of calculations can you find?

2 Within this grid there are several pairs of numbers that equal 1000.

600	500	800	330
300	510	900	730
500	200	400	350
700	480	430	680
100	210	890	550

a Find each pair that equal 1000 and colour both numbers.

b What letter of the alphabet have you coloured? [ ]

Lesson 2: **Finding the unknown number (1)**

* Find missing numbers in addition statements up to 100

1 Additions can be written in different ways.

For example, $4 + 5 = 9$ can be written as:

$$4 + 5 = 9 \qquad 5 + 4 = 9 \qquad 9 = 5 + 4 \qquad 9 = 4 + 5$$

Write each of these additions in a different way.

a $4 + 6 = 10$ _____

b $10 = 8 + 2$ _____

c $1 + 9 = 10$ _____

d $10 = 3 + 7$ _____

e $5 + 5 = 10$ _____

f $10 = 0 + 10$ _____

2 Write the unknown number in each calculation.

a $\bigcirc + 6 = 10$

b $3 + \bigcirc = 10$

c $10 = 5 + \bigcirc$

d $10 = \bigcirc + 9$

e $7 + \bigcirc = 10$

f $10 = \bigcirc + 2$

1 Write the unknown number in each calculation.

a $14 + \bigcirc = 20$

b $20 + \triangle = 30$

c $\bigcirc + 4 = 20$

d $\triangle + 15 = 30$

e $18 + \bigcirc = 20$

f $30 = 12 + \triangle$

g $20 = 15 + \bigcirc$

h $5 + \triangle = 30$

i $8 + \bigcirc = 20$

j $30 = 28 + \triangle$

Number

Number

2 Make up six unknown number questions of your own.
Write the answers in the boxes below.

My questions:

a

b

c

d

e

f

My answers:

a

b

c

d

e

f

 Challenge 3

1 Choose any two calculations. Solve them and then write a number story for each one.

$\boxed{} + 25 = 40$ $12 + \boxed{} = 40$ $5 + \boxed{} = 40$ $\boxed{} + 7 = 40$

a _____

_____

b _____

_____

2 a If 5 more than an unknown number is 50, how would you find the unknown number?

_____

b If 50 is an unknown number plus 14, how would you find the unknown number?

_____ ☹ 😐 ☺

Number

Lesson 3: **Finding the unknown number (2)**

• Find missing numbers in addition statements up to 100

Challenge 1 Each missing number in the calculation is shown on a balloon. Draw a line to match each calculation with the correct balloon.

$15 + ? = 20$ $20 = 12 + ?$ $? + 19 = 20$

8   14   5   1   10   18

$6 + ? = 20$ $20 = ? + 2$ $? + 10 = 20$

Challenge 2

1 In each triangle, the two base numbers add to make the top number.

Write the unknown number calculation. Use a question mark (?) for the unknown number.

For example:

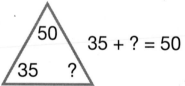

50, 35, ? $35 + ? = 50$

a

50, ?, 40

b

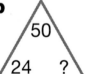

50, 24, ?

c

50, ?, 46

d

50, 34, ?

e 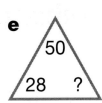 50 / 28 ? [ ]

f 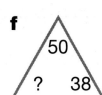 50 / ? 38 [ ]

2 For each calculation in Question 1, write the unknown number.

a [ ]   **b** [ ]   **c** [ ]

d [ ]   **e** [ ]   **f** [ ]

3 Find the missing numbers. In each question, all three calculations have the same total.

a $70 = 30 + \boxed{}$ **b** $\boxed{} + 70 = 90$ **c** $\boxed{} + 90 = 100$

$\boxed{} + 45 = 70$ $45 + \boxed{} = 90$ $100 = 45 + \boxed{}$

$62 + \boxed{} = 70$ $90 = \boxed{} + 84$ $29 + \boxed{} = 100$

 Challenge 3 'The unknown number **will always be an odd number** if the other number being added is odd and if the total is even.
For example: $? + 13 = 20$.'

    a Test this statement by trying ten different examples.

    b Look at your test calculations.
        Is the statement always true? _____

Lesson 4: **Adding pairs of 2-digit numbers**

• Add a pair of 2-digit numbers

1 Each pair of numbers is a 2-digit number that has been partitioned. What are the numbers?

For example: 50 and 6 = 56

a 40 and 1 =

b 30 and 4 =

c 20 and 4 =

d 20 and 3 =

e 20 and 2 =

f 30 and 7 =

2 Complete these calculations.

a 57 + 20 =

b 43 + 20 =

c 64 + 21 =

d 42 + 23 =

e 23 + 21 =

f 47 + 22 =

1 Complete each calculation by partitioning the second number.

For example: 46 + 25 = 46 + 20 + 5

= 66 + 5

= 71

a 57 + 26 =

=

=

b 61 + 36 =

=

=

c 35 + 27 =

=

=

d 45 + 19 =

=

=

Number

2 The table below shows the ages of children's parents. Write the total of each pair of ages in the table.

Show your working here.

	Mother's age	Father's age	Total age
Lloyd	42	40	
Mia	38	38	
Isla	37	40	
Oliver	38	45	

Challenge 3 The total of Deepa's parents' ages is 70. The difference between their ages is less than 10 years. What ages could they be?

For example:

They could be 36 and 34 because the difference between these numbers is 2 and 36 + 34 = 70.

Number

Lesson 5: **Subtracting pairs of 2-digit numbers (2)**

• Subtract one 2-digit number from another 2-digit number

Challenge 1

Complete these calculations.

a 54 – 20 = ☐

b 76 – 31 = ☐

c 36 – 11 = ☐

d 97 – 25 = ☐

e 63 – 13 = ☐

f 89 – 18 = ☐

Challenge 2

1 Complete each calculation by partitioning the second number.
For example: 57 – 34 = 57 – 30 – 4
= 27 – 4
= 23

a 79 – 24 = ☐
= ☐
= ☐

b 56 – 25 = ☐
= ☐
= ☐

c 68 – 53 = ☐
= ☐
= ☐

d 77 – 46 = ☐
= ☐
= ☐

e 94 – 62 = ☐
= ☐
= ☐

f 88 – 53 = ☐
= ☐
= ☐

Number

2 The table shows the number of fans supporting each team at a basketball tournament.

Team	Number of fans
Orange	85
Black	67
Silver	62
Purple	96
White	21
Gold	59

Subtract to find the difference between groups of fans. Remember to start with the larger number in a subtraction.

For example:
Purple and Gold

$= 96 - 59$

$= 96 - 50 - 9$

$= 46 - 9$

$= 37$

a Silver and White =   **b** Orange and White =

c Gold and Black =   **d** Purple and White =

  Challenge 3

| 1 | 2 | 3 | 4 | 5 | 6 | 7 |

Use the number cards to make four different subtraction calculations.

For example: $34 - 17 = 34 - 10 - 7$

$= 24 - 7$

$= 17$

a

b

c

d

Number

Lesson 6: **Adding 3-digit and 2-digit numbers (2)**

• Add 3-digit and 2-digit numbers together

Challenge 1

You have a counting machine with hundreds, tens and units buttons underneath.

How many times should you press the tens and units buttons to add these numbers?

For example:
565 + 23 = 565 + 2 tens + 3 units

a 732 + 46 = [   ] + [   ] tens + [   ] units

b 426 + 31 = [   ] + [   ] tens + [   ] units

c 374 + 23 = [   ] + [   ] tens + [   ] units

d 502 + 67 = [   ] + [   ] tens + [   ] units

Challenge 2

1 Work out each word problem. Show your working in the boxes.

For example: What is the sum of 539 and 38?

$$539 + 38 = 539 + 30 + 8$$
$$= 569 + 8$$
$$= 577$$

a What is the total of 358 and 53?

[   ]

b There are 617 people at a sporting event. Another 45 people turn up. How many people are now at the event?

c How much is $508 and $69 altogether?

2 Only two of the calculations are correct. Tick them.

a $424 + 59 = 479$ ☐

b $368 + 24 = 382$ ☐

c $531 + 98 = 629$ ☐

d $743 + 53 = 796$ ☐

Challenge 3 Maisie makes an addition using the digits 1, 4, 5, 7 and 3. To estimate the answers, she rounds her numbers and adds $750 + 40 = 790$.

a What could her numbers be? ☐ + ☐

b Work out the actual answer to the calculation you have written. Show your working in the box.

Lesson 7: **Adding and subtracting a single-digit number to and from a 3-digit number**

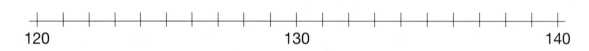

• Add and subtract single-digit numbers to and from 3-digit numbers

Number (side tab)

 1 Use the number line to help answer these calculations.

```
+--+--+--+--+--+--+--+--+--+--+--+--+--+--+--+--+--+--+--+--+
120              130              140
```

a 139 − 6 = [ ]   **b** 122 + 3 = [ ]

c 139 − 5 = [ ]   **d** 121 + 7 = [ ]

e 125 + 4 = [ ]   **f** 131 + 3 = [ ]

2 (0)   (2)   (4)   (6)   (8)

Each of these calculations ends in an even digit. Write the even digit in the box.

a 142 + 6 = 14[ ]   **b** 127 − 7 = 12[ ]   **c** 134 − 4 = 13[ ]

d 137 − 3 = 13[ ]   **e** 130 + 2 = 13[ ]   **f** 138 − 6 = 13[ ]

 1 Complete these calculations.

a 526 + 9 = [ ]   **b** 490 − 3 = [ ]

c [ ] + 4 = 672   **d** [ ] − 5 = 204

e [ ] = 644 + 8   **f** [ ] = 139 − 5

2 Children guess the number of sweets in their jars. Work out the actual number of sweets.

For example:
Claire thinks there are 284 sweets in her jar. This is 6 more than the actual amount. How many sweets are in Claire's jar?

284 – 6 = 278 sweets   284 is 6 more than 278

a Asim thinks there are 142 sweets in his jar. This is 7 more than the actual amount. How many sweets are in Asim's jar?

b Jody thinks there are 578 sweets in her jar. This is 2 less than the actual amount. How many sweets are in Jody's jar?

 Use these number cards to make three HTU + U additions and three HTU – U subtractions.

| 5 | 2 | 9 | 9 | 3 | 8 | 5 |

Additions:

a   **b**   **c**

Subtractions:

d   **e**   **f**

Number

Lesson 8: **Adding and subtracting multiples of 10 and 100 to and from 3-digit numbers**

• Find 20, 30,... 90, 100, 200, 300 more and less than 3-digit numbers

Challenge 1

1 Use the number line to help you find the totals of these numbers.

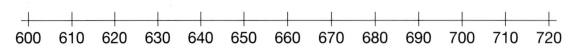

600 610 620 630 640 650 660 670 680 690 700 710 720

a $640 + 50 =$ ⬜

b $660 + 30 =$ ⬜

c $630 + 20 =$ ⬜

d $610 + 90 =$ ⬜

2 Use the number line to help you subtract these numbers.

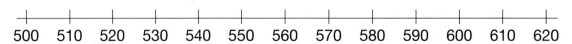

500 510 520 530 540 550 560 570 580 590 600 610 620

a $590 - 50 =$ ⬜

b $540 - 30 =$ ⬜

c $620 - 60 =$ ⬜

d $570 - 40 =$ ⬜

Challenge 2

1 Write out the calculation then work out the answer.

For example: What is 50 less than 431? $431 - 50 = 381$

a What is 30 more than 359? ⬜

b What is 100 less than 425? ⬜

c What is 60 less than 182? ⬜

d What is 200 more than 295? ⬜

2 Ten people visit a bank and either put money in or take money out. Work out the amount of money each person now has.

Person	How much do they have in the bank to start with?	What do they do?	What is the calculation?	What is their new balance?
Example	$357	Take out $40	357 − 40	$317
A	$134	Take out $30		
B	$106	Put in $90		
C	$230	Take out $40		
D	$581	Put in $300		

3 Complete these statements with the letters A–D. Use the table in Question 2 to help.

a Person ☐ has the most money now.

b Person ☐ has the least money now.

Challenge 3 Use the box to draw a picture or sketch a number line to help solve the problem.

Lucy has 158 old coins in her collection.
She is given another 60 coins. She decides to give 90 coins from her collection to her sister.

How many coins does Lucy now have?

Lucy now has ☐ coins.   ☹ 😐 ☺

Number

Lesson 1:Multiplication and division facts for 2×, 3×, 5× and 10× tables (1)

• Recall multiplication and division facts for 2×, 3×, 5× and 10× tables

Challenge 1

1 Count in 2s and complete the chains.

a | 2 | 4 | 6 | | | | 14 | | 18 | |

b | 20 | 18 | | | | 10 | | | 4 | |

2 Count in 5s and complete the chains.

a | 5 | 10 | | | 25 | 30 | | | | |

b | | | | | | | 20 | 15 | | |

Challenge 2

1 Complete these multiplication grids.

a

×	4	2	9
2			
10			

b

×	6	5	8
2			
10			

c

×	7	10	6
3			
5			

d

×	3	8	9
3			
5			

2 Use your knowledge of times-table and division facts to work out the missing numbers.

×	A	B	C
3	21	D	18
5	E	15	30
10	70	F	G

A = ☐   B = ☐   C = ☐   D = ☐

E = ☐   F = ☐   G = ☐

Number

3 a Mara has seven $5 notes. How much money does she have in total?

She has $ ☐.

b Jessica has 30 spellings to learn. She splits them equally over 10 days before her test. How many spellings does she learn each day?

She learns ☐ spellings per day.

c On a class trip to the beach, 18 children are split into groups of 2. How many groups of 2 are there?

There are ☐ groups.

1 Work out the numbers being multiplied by looking carefully at each row and column. Write down the numbers that each letter represents.

×	A	B	C	D
E	12	10	18	14
F	60	50	90	70
G	30	25	45	35
H	18	15	27	21

A = ☐   B = ☐   C = ☐

D = ☐   E = ☐   F = ☐

G = ☐   H = ☐

2 Design a similar puzzle for your friends to try.

×	A	B	C	D
E				
F				
G				
H				

A = ☐   B = ☐   C = ☐

D = ☐   E = ☐   F = ☐

G = ☐   H = ☐

☹ 😐 ☺

Number

Lesson 2: **Multiplication and division facts for 2×, 3×, 5× and 10× tables (2)**

• Recall multiplication and division facts for 2×, 3×, 5× and 10× tables

 Challenge 1

1 Draw a line to match each 2× table with the correct answer.

| 4 × 2 | 6 × 2 | 3 × 2 | 9 × 2 | 10 × 2 | 7 × 2 |

| 20 | 6 | 12 | 14 | 18 | 8 |

2 Draw a line to match each 10× table with the correct answer.

| 6 × 10 | 2 × 10 | 8 × 10 | 5 × 10 | 7 × 10 | 9 × 10 |

| 90 | 60 | 70 | 80 | 50 | 20 |

Challenge 2

1 Complete these multiplication targets.

The first number has been completed each time as an example.

a
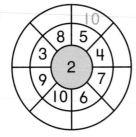

b
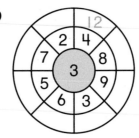

2 You will need to use division to complete these next two targets.

a
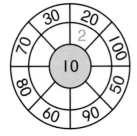

b
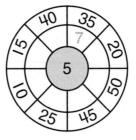

3 First work out the middle number, then complete the rest of this target.

4 Complete these calculations.

  a $9 \times 5 = \boxed{}$ **b** $10 \times 3 = \boxed{}$ **c** $30 \div 5 = \boxed{}$

  d $1 \times 2 = \boxed{}$ **e** $18 \div 2 = \boxed{}$ **f** $70 \div 10 = \boxed{}$

Challenge 3

1 Only two of these word problems are multiplication or division questions.

  a Connor has to wait 35 minutes until his bus arrives. He talks to his friend for 12 minutes. How long does he have left?

  b Erin gives 24 sweets to 3 of her friends, so that all 3 have the same amount. How many sweets does each of her friends have?

  c There are 26 people on a bus. At the next village another 14 people get on. How many people are now on the bus?

  d Jermaine saves $5 every week. How much money will he have saved in 6 weeks?

  Which two questions do you need to multiply or divide to answer?

  $\boxed{}$ and $\boxed{}$

2 Use the boxes below to answer the two questions you chose.

  Draw a diagram to show the word problem if it helps.

Number

Lesson 3: **Multiplication and division facts for the 4× table (1)**

- Recall the 4× tables facts

 Challenge 1

Fill in each multiple of 4 in this number square. Then colour all of the multiples of 4.

1	2	3		5	6	7		9	10
11		13	14	15		17	18	19	
21	22	23		25	26	27		29	30
31		33	34	35		37	38	39	

Challenge 2

1 This table shows the number of cars that came to the garage during a week and the total number of tyres that needed to be changed.

a Fill in the missing numbers.

Speedy Garage			
Day	**Number of cars**	**Number of tyres per car**	**Total number of tyres changed**
Monday	5	4	20
Tuesday	2	4	
Wednesday	7	4	
Thursday		4	36
Friday	4	4	
Saturday		4	24

b How many tyres are there on 10 cars? ☐ tyres

c The garage changed 12 tyres. How many cars is that? ☐ cars

d Tomorrow the garage has 9 cars booked in. How many tyres will they need? ☐ tyres

2 Complete these calculations.

a 8 × 4 = ☐

b 2 × 4 = ☐

c 40 ÷ 4 = ☐

d 3 × 4 = ☐

e 24 ÷ 4 = ☐

f 20 ÷ 4 = ☐

Number

3 a What are five fours? ☐

b How many fours are in 12? ☐

c What is the product of 10 and 4? ☐

d What is 28 split into four? ☐

Challenge 3

1 a Write out the multiples of 4, from 4 to 40, in order.

☐ ☐ ☐ ☐ ☐ ☐ ☐ ☐ ☐ ☐

b Underline the units digit in each number.

c Look carefully at the units digits you have underlined. Is there a pattern in the numbers?

_____

2 Use the pattern you have found to predict the multiples of 4 that come after the number 40.

☹ 😐 ☺

Number

Lesson 4: **Multiplication and division facts for the 4× table (2)**

- Recall the 4× tables facts

You will need
- coloured pencils

1 a Draw 3 groups of 4 dots.

How many dots altogether?

b Draw 7 groups of 4 dots.

How many dots altogether?

c Draw 5 groups of 4 dots.

How many dots altogether?

2 Colour each of these 4× tables questions and their answers. Use the same colour for each pair.

| 5 × 4 | 2 × 4 | 40 ÷ 4 | 12 ÷ 4 | 4 × 4 | 24 ÷ 4 |

| 6 | 3 | 20 | 16 | 8 | 10 |

1 Double each of these numbers twice to find the 4× tables facts.

Example: 3 ➡ 6 ➡ 12   So 3 × 4 = 12

a 5 ➡ ⬜ ➡ ⬜   So ⬜ × 4 = ⬜

b 2 ➡ ⬜ ➡ ⬜   So ⬜ × 4 = ⬜

c 7 ➡ ⬜ ➡ ⬜   So ⬜ × 4 = ⬜

d 4 ➡ ⬜ ➡ ⬜   So ⬜ × 4 = ⬜

Number

2 Complete these calculations.

a 6 × 4 = ☐   **b** 28 ÷ 4 = ☐   **c** 5 × 4 = ☐

d 32 ÷ 4 = ☐   **e** 4 × 4 = ☐   **f** 36 ÷ 4 = ☐

3 a What are seven groups of four? ☐

b What is 20 shared into four? ☐

c What is the product of 6 and 4? ☐

d How many fours are in 40? ☐

Challenge 3

1 Multiply the numbers in the squares together and write the answers in the circles between the squares.

For example:

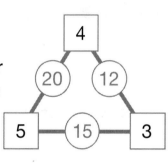

a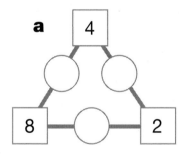

b

c

2 Use your knowledge of division facts to help fill in the squares.

a

b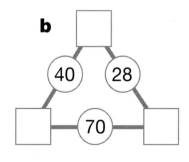

c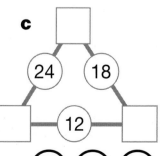

☹ 😐 ☺

113

Number

Lesson 5: **Multiples of 2, 5 and 10**

• Recognise 2- and 3-digit multiples of 2, 5 and 10

Challenge 1

1 Colour the multiples of 2.

(36) (60) (73) (21) (52) (59) (28) (37) (44) (72) (15) (16) (30) (23) (66)

2 a Circle the correct word.
All multiples of 2 are odd / even numbers.

b Complete the sentence.
All multiples of 2 end in ☐ , ☐ , ☐ , ☐ or ☐ .

Challenge 2

1 Circle the multiples of 5 in each list.

a 275   520   898   **b** 344   600   425

c 479   552   895   **d** 385   212   401

2 Circle the multiples of 10 in each list.

a 703   890   401   **b** 400   827   570

c 250   310   258   **d** 565   700   450

3 Abdul says, 'My number has three digits. It is a multiple of 10 and is larger than 425.'

a Can his number be 537? Circle your answer. Yes / No
Explain your answer.

_____

_____

b Can his number be 340? Circle your answer. Yes / No
Explain your answer.

_____

_____

Number

c Is Abdul's number a multiple of 5? Circle your answer.

Yes / No

Explain your answer.

_____

_____

d Write three numbers that Abdul's number could be.

Challenge 3

1 Complete the table by writing the nearest multiples of 10, 5 and 2 to each number.

Number	Nearest multiple of 10	Nearest multiple of 5	Nearest multiple of 2
247	250	245	246 or 248
368			
474			
883			
557			

2 Jared says he has found a 3-digit number for which the nearest multiple of 10, the nearest multiple of 5 and the nearest multiple of 2 are all the same.

Can you find any numbers for which this is true?

☹ 😐 ☺

Lesson 6: **Halving and doubling (1)**

• Understand the links between halving and doubling numbers

1 Write the number that is half of each given number.

   a Half of 4 is ☐.   **b** Half of 10 is ☐.

   c Half of 12 is ☐.   **d** Half of 8 is ☐.

   e Half of 20 is ☐.   **f** Half of 16 is ☐.

2 Write the number that is double each given number.

   a Double 3 is ☐.   **b** Double 7 is ☐.

   c Double 4 is ☐.   **d** Double 10 is ☐.

   e Double 8 is ☐.   **f** Double 9 is ☐.

Challenge 2

1 The number on each balloon is equal to a number on one of the boxes at the bottom. Draw lines to match the pairs.

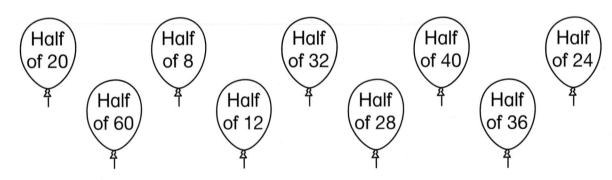

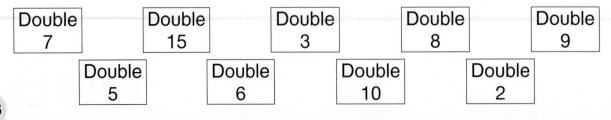

Number

2 Complete these doubling chains.

a

b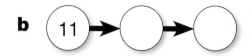

c

d

3 Complete these halving chains.

a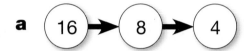

b

c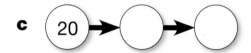

d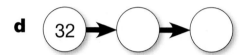

 Challenge 3

1 a Aimee picks a 2-digit number card and doubles the number. Her answer is 32. What was her number?

b Aimee picks another number card and halves the number. Her answer is 43. What was her number?

c Aimee picks a third number card and doubles the number. Her answer is 68. What was her number?

d Explain how to answer questions like these.

_____

_____

2 Write two halving or doubling questions of your own for a friend to solve.

a _____

_____

b _____

_____

117

Number

Lesson 7: **Multiplying 2-digit numbers by 10**

- Multiply 2-digit numbers by 10

 Challenge 1 Multiply numbers by 10.

a

$2 \times 10 = \boxed{}$

b

$3 \times 10 = \boxed{}$

c

$5 \times 10 = \boxed{}$

d

$6 \times 10 = \boxed{}$

Challenge 2

1 Jamila has a set of digit cards and makes 2-digit numbers with them. She multiplies each number by 10 by shifting each digit one place to the left. Show how the position of each digit changes.

Example:

H	T	U
	1	2
1	2	0

So $12 \times 10 = 120$

a

H	T	U
	2	8

b

H	T	U
	5	2

c

H	T	U
	9	6

So $\boxed{} \times 10 = \boxed{}$

So $\boxed{} \times 10 = \boxed{}$

So $\boxed{} \times 10 = \boxed{}$

d Your answers to these questions are all multiples of 10. What do you notice about all multiples of 10?

_____

_____

Number

2 These children are saving different amounts every week. How much will each one have saved after 10 weeks?

	Amount saved each week	Amount saved after 10 weeks
Harrison	$12	$120
Jade	$16	
Kyle	$11	
Lauren	$23	

Challenge 3

1 Rashida takes two digit cards and makes two different 2-digit numbers. She multiplies both numbers by 10. Her first answer is between 200 and 300. Her second answer is between 600 and 700.

a What were the numbers on Rashida's cards? ☐ and ☐

b What were the two calculations she made?

☐ × 10 = ☐ and ☐ × 10 = ☐

2 Rashida takes two more digit cards and makes two different 2-digit numbers. She multiplies both numbers by 10. Her first answer is between 500 and 600. The sum of the digits in the second answer is 12.

a What were the numbers on Rashida's cards? ☐ and ☐

b What were the two calculations she made?

☐ × 10 = ☐ and ☐ × 10 = ☐

119

Lesson 8: **Multiplication in any order**

* Multiply numbers in any order and understand the answer will be the same

 1 Draw lines to join the matching multiplications.

a 4 × 5 •	• 2 × 3
b 3 × 2 •	• 10 × 5
c 5 × 10 •	• 5 × 2
d 2 × 5 •	• 5 × 4

2 Multiplications can be worked out in any order. Write the answers to the multiplication pairs you made in Question 1.

a ☐ **b** ☐ **c** ☐ **d** ☐

 1 Draw each of these multiplications in two different ways. Then write the answer in the box.

a 7 × 3 or 3 × 7

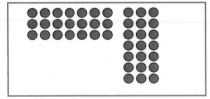

= 21

b 3 × 4 or 4 × 3

= ☐

c 4 × 6 or 6 × 4

= ☐

d 4 × 5 or 5 × 4

= ☐

Number

2 Write the missing numbers to show that multiplication can be done in any order.

a $8 \times 5 = 5 \times \boxed{8} = \boxed{40}$

b $6 \times 3 = \boxed{} \times \boxed{} = \boxed{}$

c $7 \times 2 = 2 \times \boxed{} = \boxed{}$

d $4 \times 10 = 10 \times \boxed{} = \boxed{}$

e $9 \times 5 = \boxed{} \times 9 = \boxed{}$

f $8 \times 2 = \boxed{} \times 8 = \boxed{}$

g $3 \times 9 = \boxed{} \times 3 = \boxed{}$

h $10 \times 9 = \boxed{} \times \boxed{} = \boxed{}$

Challenge 3

Kayleigh wants to test the idea that multiplication can be done in any order, so she tries multiplying three numbers in different orders.

Example:

$2 \times 3 \times 5 = 2 \times 3 \times 5$	$2 \times 3 \times 5 = 2 \times 5 \times 3$	$2 \times 3 \times 5 = 5 \times 3 \times 2$
$= 6 \times 5$	$= 10 \times 3$	$= 15 \times 2$
$= 30$	$= 30$	$= 30$

Look carefully at Kayleigh's example. She says that it shows that multiplication works in any order, no matter how many numbers you are multiplying.

a Is Kayleigh's idea correct? Yes / No

b Why do you think this? _____

_____

_____

c Test Kayleigh's idea for yourself below. First, work out a multiplication one way, then rearrange the numbers to see whether the answer is the same.

You could try multiplying four numbers!

121

Lesson 1: **Multiplication and division facts for 2×, 3×, 4×, 5× and 10× tables (1)**

- Recall multiplication and division facts for the 2×, 3×, 4×, 5× and 10× tables

Challenge 1

1 Draw 4 dots in each square and write the total as you go along.

•• ••	•• ••							
4	8							

2 Draw a line to match each 4× table with the correct answer.

4 × 4   2 × 4   3 × 4   9 × 4   10 × 4   7 × 4   5 × 4

20   16   28   8   12   40   36

3 Draw a line to match each division with the correct answer.

40 ÷ 4   16 ÷ 4   4 ÷ 4   32 ÷ 4   20 ÷ 4   12 ÷ 4   24 ÷ 4

5   10   6   3   1   8   4

Challenge 2

1 Complete these.

a Multiply 4 by itself ☐

b 5 × 10 = ☐

c 7 × 5 = ☐

d What are nine 3s? ☐

e Double 10 = ☐

f 7 × 3 = ☐

g 3 × 3 = ☐

h 5 × 5 = ☐

i What are 6 lots of 5? ☐

2 Complete these.

a 24 ÷ 4 = ☐

b 40 ÷ 4 = ☐

c How many fives in 20? ☐

d 40 ÷ 5 = ☐

e 70 ÷ 10 = ☐

f What is half of 18? ☐

g 18 ÷ 2 = ☐

h 45 ÷ 5 = ☐

3 Use your knowledge of each times table to complete the multiplication squares.

a

×	3	10	4
2			
10			
4			

b

×	2	5	4
3			
10			
5			

Challenge 3

1 Work out what each letter represents.

×	A	B	C
D	15	50	10
E	12	40	8
F	30	100	20

A = ☐ B = ☐

C = ☐ D = ☐

E = ☐ F = ☐

2 Rachel has 18 flowers to plant.

She digs an odd number of rows and plants an even number of flowers in each row. Draw how Rachel's flowers could be arranged.

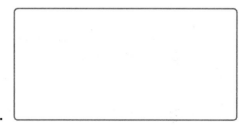

18 = ☐ rows each containing ☐ flowers.

Number

Lesson 2: **Doubles of numbers to 20 and related halves**

• Double numbers up to 20 and find half of the answer

Challenge 1

Double each amount and write the total number in the answer box.

a

[ ] circles

b

[ ] triangles

c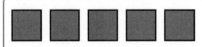

[ ] squares

d

[ ] stars

Challenge 2

1 Complete these statements.

a Double 6 = [ ]   **b** Double 2 = [ ]

c Double 11 = [ ]   **d** Double 12 = [ ]

e Double 16 = [ ]   **f** Double 9 = [ ]

g Double 4 = [ ]   **h** Double 13 = [ ]

i Double 20 = [ ]   **j** Double 3 = [ ]

2 Draw lines to match the doubles and halves that are equal.

Double 5 •   • Half of 48

Double 12 •   • Half of 40

Double 9 •   • Half of 20

Double 8 •   • Half of 32

Double 10 •   • Half of 36

3 a Maya thinks of a number and doubles it.

She gets 34. What was her number?

b Zac thinks of a number and doubles it.

He gets 26. What was his number?

Challenge 3

1 There are two numbers that end in a 6 between 1 and 20. They are 6 and 16. Double both numbers. What is the same about both of them? _____

2 The double of any number that ends in the digit 6 will always end in the digit 2.

Why is this? _____

3 What will happen if you double any number that ends in a 7?

_____

4 What will happen if you double any number that ends in an 8?

_____

5 Sam makes a 2-digit number using the digits: 1, 3, 4, 5 and 6. He doubles it. Sam says that his answer ends in a 4. Is this possible? Why? / why not?

_____

_____

_____

☹ 😐 ☺

Lesson 3: **Doubles of multiples of 5 and related halves**

Number

• Double multiples of 5 and find half of the answer

 1 **a** Colour the multiples of 5 in the number grid.

1	2	3	4	5	6	7	8	9	10
11	12	13	14	15	16	17	18	19	20
21	22	23	24	25	26	27	28	29	30
31	32	33	34	35	36	37	38	39	40
41	42	43	44	45	46	47	48	49	50

b What do you notice about all the numbers in the 5 times table?

_____

c If the grid was bigger, what would be the next two multiples of 5?

☐ and ☐

 1 Complete these statements.

a Double 30 = ☐   **b** Half of 20 = ☐

c Double 75 = ☐   **d** Half of 200 = ☐

e Double 25 = ☐   **f** Half of 30 = ☐

g Double 85 = ☐   **h** Half of 180 = ☐

2 The table shows the heights of the different office blocks.

a Use doubling or halving to fill in the missing numbers.
The first row has been completed for you as an example.

Name of company	Halfway height	Total height
IT Computers	15 floors	30 floors
NRG Electricity	20 floors	
LO Mobile Phones	35 floors	
YOY Complaints		50 floors
IOU Bank		90 floors

b Look at the Total height column. What can you say about all multiples of 5 when they are doubled?

_____

Challenge 3

Mia thinks she has found a quick way to double multiples of 5 that end in 5. She says: 'First, I round the number down to the nearest 10. Then I double that number because doubling multiples of 10 is easier. Then I add 10 to the answer.'

a Try some examples in the box below.

b Does Mia's method work? ☐

c Yasmin says to Mia: 'You don't round numbers that end in 5 down, you round them up!'
How could Mia change her method so that it still works if she rounds the numbers up?

_____

☹ 😐 ☺

127

Number

Lesson 4: **Multiplying single-digit numbers by 2, 3, 4, 5, 6, 9 and 10 (1)**

• Multiply a single-digit number by 2, 3, 4, 5, 6, 9 or 10

Challenge 1

1 a Draw 3 groups of 6 dots.

How many have dots you drawn altogether?

b Draw 2 groups of 9 dots.

How many dots have you drawn altogether?

2 Draw a line to match each 6× table calculation with the correct answer.

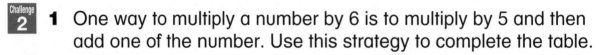

| 1×6 | 2×6 | 3×6 | 4×6 | 5×6 | 6×6 |

| 54 | 36 | 6 | 30 | 60 | 12 | 48 | 18 | 24 | 42 |

| 7×6 | 8×6 | 9×6 | 10×6 |

Challenge 2

1 One way to multiply a number by 6 is to multiply by 5 and then add one of the number. Use this strategy to complete the table.

	Multiply by 5	Add one of the number	And so...
4	$4 \times 5 = 20$	$20 + 4 = 24$	$4 \times 6 = 24$
2			
7			
9			
3			
6			
5			
8			
10			

2 One way to multiply a number by 9 is to multiply by 10 and then subtract one of the number.
Use this strategy to complete the table.

	Multiply by 10	**Subtract one less of the number**	**And so...**
6	$6 \times 10 = 60$	$60 - 6 = 54$	$9 \times 6 = 54$
4			
9			
3			
7			
8			

3 Fill in the answers.

a 2 groups of 6 = ☐   **b** $6 \times 5 = $ ☐

c 8 lots of 10 = ☐   **d** $6 \times 6 = $ ☐

e $5 \times 2 = $ ☐   **f** Eight 3s = ☐

1 Rhian wants to print out 8 copies of her story. It is 9 pages long. How many pieces of paper does she need?

☐ pieces of paper

2 Sam has scored 3 goals in every game he has played this season. So far, he has played 6 games. How many more goals will he need to score to get to 20?

☐ more goals

3 Hassan takes 4 digit cards and uses them to make 2 multiplications. Both multiplications give the answer 12.

What are Hassan's digits? ☐ ☐ ☐ ☐

Lesson 5: **Multiplying single-digit numbers by 2, 3, 4, 5, 6, 9 and 10 (2)**

- Multiply a single-digit number by 2, 3, 4, 5, 6, 9 or 10

You will need
- coloured pencils

Challenge 1

1 Use the number lines to answer the questions.

a
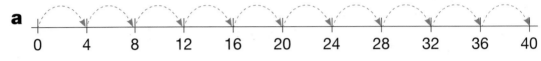

0   4   8   12   16   20   24   28   32   36   40

2 jumps = 4 × 2 = ☐   7 jumps = 4 × 7 = ☐

9 jumps = 4 × 9 = ☐

b
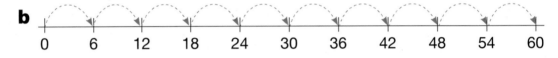

0   6   12   18   24   30   36   42   48   54   60

3 jumps = 6 × 3 = ☐   5 jumps = 6 × 5 = ☐

8 jumps = 6 × 8 = ☐

2 Colour each of these 9× tables questions and their answers. Use the same colour for each pair.

| 1 × 9 | 2 × 9 | 3 × 9 | 4 × 9 | 5 × 9 |

| 6 × 9 | 7 × 9 | 8 × 9 | 9 × 9 | 10 × 9 |

81   72   54   45   18   90   9   36   63   27

Challenge 2

1 Draw the jumps on each blank number line, then write the correct answers.

a ├─────────────────────────────────┤

7 × 9 = ☐

b ├─────────────────────────────────┤

8 × 3 = ☐

c

$7 \times 4 = \boxed{}$

d

$8 \times 5 = \boxed{}$

2 Fill in the answers.

a $7 \times 6 = \boxed{}$ **b** 4 doubled $= \boxed{}$

c Product of 2 and 5 $= \boxed{}$ **d** $5 \times 5 = \boxed{}$

e $9 \times 2 = \boxed{}$ **f** $10 \times 2 = \boxed{}$ **g** $7 \times 3 = \boxed{}$

h 3 times 6 $= \boxed{}$ **i** 6 groups of 4 $= \boxed{}$ **j** $3 \times 9 = \boxed{}$

k $9 \times 10 = \boxed{}$ **l** 10 lots of 10 $= \boxed{}$ **m** $5 \times 6 = \boxed{}$

n $8 \times 4 = \boxed{}$ **o** $10 \times 4 = \boxed{}$ **p** $6 \times 8 = \boxed{}$

Challenge 3

1 Use the numbers already given as clues to help complete the multiplication grid.

×	8			
		15		45
		9	6	
	48	18		
	16		4	18

2 Use the numbers already given as clues to help complete the multiplication grid.

×				
	3			27
	5	20		
9			90	81
		16	40	

Number

Lesson 6: **Dividing 2-digit numbers by 2, 3, 4, 5, 6, 9 and 10 (1)**

• Divide a 2-digit number by 2, 3, 4, 5, 6, 9 or 10

1 Share 20 counters equally between 4.

   a Draw the groups of counters.

   b How many counters are there in each group? ☐

2 Share 27 counters equally between 3.

   a Draw the groups of counters.

   b How many counters are there in each group? ☐

1 Fill in the answers.

   a $16 \div 4 =$ ☐   **b** $18 \div 2 =$ ☐

   c $45 \div 5 =$ ☐   **d** $30 \div 6 =$ ☐

   e $45 \div 9 =$ ☐   **f** $90 \div 10 =$ ☐

   g Half of $12 =$ ☐   **h** $35 \div 5 =$ ☐

   i $12 \div 3 =$ ☐   **j** $27 \div 9 =$ ☐

2 Use drawings to help you work out the answers to these problems.

   a Becky saves $6 every week. How many weeks will it take her to save $42?

       weeks

   b There are 40 cars in a car park. They are parked in rows of 10. How many rows are there?

       rows

   c There are 9 chocolate bars in a packet. Joe needs to buy 45 bars. How many packets should he buy?

       packets

   d 27 comics are split equally among 3 friends. How many comics do they have each?

       comics

Challenge 3

1 Athan has an even number of counters. He shares them equally between 3 and has 1 counter left over. How many counters do you think Athan had to start with?

2 Naveed has an odd number of DVDs. He splits them into equal piles of 10 and has 2 DVDs left over. Why is this impossible?

                                     ☹ 😐 ☺

Number

Lesson 7: **Dividing 2-digit numbers by 2, 3, 4, 5, 6, 9 and 10 (2)**

• Divide a 2-digit number by 2, 3, 4, 5, 6, 9 or 10

Challenge 1 Count the jumps backwards from each number to help answer the questions.

a

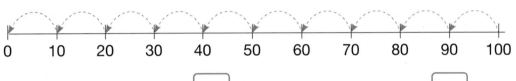

How many 10s in 70? ☐   How many 10s in 90? ☐

b

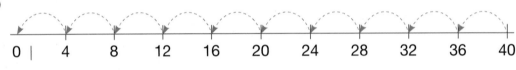

How many 4s in 32? ☐   How many 4s in 24? ☐

Challenge 2

1 Use your knowledge of division to fill in the top row of numbers.

a

×					
3	12	30	24	21	27

b

×					
5	35	15	40	5	25

c

×					
6	18	12	30	42	54

d

×					
10	100	50	30	70	90

e

×					
9	81	54	90	36	45

f

×					
2	14	4	16	18	20

2 Fill in the answers.

a 20 shared between 4 = ☐   **b** 50 ÷ 10 = ☐

c 30 ÷ 10 = ☐   **d** Half of 14 = ☐

Number

3 These calculations will not divide equally. Find the answer and write how many are left over. The first one has been done as an example.

a 17 ÷ 3 = | 5 with 2 left over |

b 9 ÷ 2 = | |

c 22 ÷ 5 = | |

d 48 ÷ 9 = | |

1 Class 3 are looking closely at division questions to see whether they can spot any patterns.
Imran has been looking at dividing numbers by 2 and also by 4. The table shows what he has written.

	÷ 2	÷ 4
12	6	3
40	20	10
24	12	6
8	4	2
16	8	4

Compare each of the ÷ 2 answers with the ÷ 4 answers. What do you notice?

_____

_____

_____

2 Complete these calculations. Some of the them will not divide equally. Write any remainders in the box.

a 37 ÷ 6 = | 6 with a remainder of 1 |

b 96 ÷ 10 = | |

c 65 ÷ 5 = | |

d 42 ÷ 3 = | |

e 19 ÷ 4 = | |

f 81 ÷ 9 = | |

☹ 😐 ☺

135

Number

Lesson 8: **Linking multiplication and division**

- Understand how multiplication and division are linked
- Write related multiplication and division facts

You will need
- coloured pencils

 1 Shade each pair of related multiplication and division facts the same colour.

$2 \times 4 = 8$	$8 \times 3 = 24$	$6 \times 6 = 36$	$7 \times 9 = 63$
$5 \times 2 = 10$	$10 \times 4 = 40$	$63 \div 9 = 7$	$10 \div 2 = 5$
$8 \div 2 = 4$	$40 \div 10 = 4$	$36 \div 6 = 6$	$24 \div 3 = 8$

2 Complete the multiplication and division fact for each array.

a

$3 \times 5 = \boxed{}$

$15 \div 3 = \boxed{}$

b

$6 \times 4 = \boxed{}$

$24 \div 4 = \boxed{}$

c

$9 \times 2 = \boxed{}$

$18 \div 9 = \boxed{}$

 1 Write a multiplication and division fact for each triangle.

a

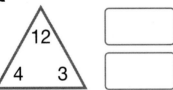

b

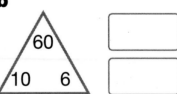

c

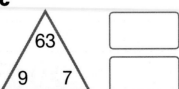

d

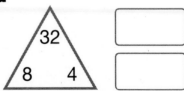

2 Use multiplication to answer these division questions.
For example: How many 6s in 42? $7 \times 6 = 42$

a How many 9s in 72?

☐ $\times 9 = 72$

b How many 3s in 21?

☐ $\times 3 = 21$

c How many 2s in 20?

☐ $\times 2 = 20$

d How many 6s in 30?

☐ $\times 6 = 30$

Challenge 3

1 Tariq takes 16 cubes. He makes 3 different rectangles with them and writes down 5 different multiplication and division facts. Can you beat his score? Write your multiplication and division facts in the box. Try rearranging 16 cubes on the table or drawing them if it helps.

2 Tariq takes 13 cubes.

Can he make any rectangles or write any multiplication or division facts about this number? Explain why you think this.

_____

_____

Number

Lesson 1: **Multiplication and division facts for 2×, 3×, 4×, 5× and 10× tables (2)**

- Recall multiplication and division facts for the 2×, 3×, 4×, 5× and 10× tables

1 Draw a line to match each addition with the multiplication. Then write the answer in each box.

a 2 + 2 + 2 + 2 •   • 3 × 10 = ☐

b 10 + 10 + 10 •   • 4 × 3 = ☐

c 5 + 5 + 5 •   • 3 × 5 = ☐

d 3 + 3 + 3 + 3 •   • 4 × 2 = ☐

2 a    **b**

How many 2s are in 18? ☐

How many 4s are in 12? ☐

1 a Complete the multiplication grid.

×	10	4	3
2			
5			
7			

b Write a division fact for six of the numbers in the grid you have completed.

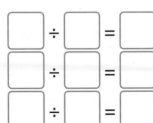

2 Class 3 hold a cake sale. The table shows the total amount of money each person makes.

a Complete the table.

Name	Number of cakes sold	Price of cakes (in $)	Total (in $)
Sacha		$2	$16
Thomas	8	$3	
Uday		$3	$27
Will		$2	$12

b Who made the most money?

c One of the children made twice as much money as someone else. Who was that person?

Challenge 3

1 Fill in the squares of this multiplication grid.

×	5		4	2	
	35				
10		30			100
			24		
				16	

2 Choose a fact from the grid and write a number story for it.

Fact = _____

_____

_____

_____

_____

_____

☹ 😐 ☺

Number

Lesson 2: **Halving and doubling (2)**

- Double numbers up to 20 and multiples of 5 less than 100 and halve the answers

You will need
- coloured pencils

Challenge 1

1 Each of the numbers in the squares has been made by doubling one of the numbers in the circles.

Colour each pair the same colour to show the doubles.

3	6	1	5	2	4
8	2	6	12	10	4

2 Colour in half of these amounts.

a ☐☐☐☐☐☐☐☐☐☐   Half of 10 is ☐.

b ○○○○○○○○   Half of 8 is ☐.

Challenge 2

1 Use these numbers to write five different halving and doubling facts, based on the numbers.

32	45	50	35	14
8	25	90	16	70

Example: Half of 32 is 16

```
[                    ]
[                    ]
[                    ]
[                    ]
[                    ]
```

2 Each of the numbers on the outside ring of this target board is double the number on the inside ring. Complete the target board.

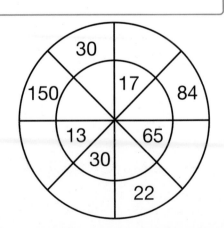

3 Ryan says 'Double 7 is the same as half of 28.'
This sentence is true because both answers are 14.
Complete each of these sentences.

a Double 20 is the same as half of ☐.

b Double ☐ is the same as half of 16.

c Double 3 is the same as half of ☐.

d Double ☐ is the same as half of 20.

Challenge 3

| 1 | 6 | 5 | 4 |

a Jamie uses these digit cards to make a 2-digit number, then doubles it. He says that the answer ends in a 2.
Write a doubling fact that Jamie could have made.

_____

b Jamie makes another 2-digit number from the same digit cards and doubles it. He says that the answer ends in a 6.
Isla says that this is impossible. Why is Isla correct?

_____

_____

c Isla uses the digit cards to make a 2-digit number and doubles it. Will her answer be an odd number?
Explain why / why not.

_____

_____

☹ 😐 ☺

141

Number

Lesson 3: **Doubling multiples of 50**

• Double multiples of 50 to 500

Challenge 1

1 a Fill in the multiples of 50.

50, 100, 150, [ ] , [ ] , [ ] , [ ] , [ ] , [ ] , 500

b What do you notice about all the numbers you have written?

_____

c If the pattern continued past 500, what would the next three multiples of 50 be? [ ] , [ ] , [ ]

2 Complete these doubles.

a Double 100 = [ ]   **b** Double 300 = [ ]

c Double 200 = [ ]   **d** Double 400 = [ ]

Challenge 2

1 Show how these numbers can be doubled by partitioning.

Example:

Double 250 — Double 200 = 400 — 400 + 100 = 500
— Double 50 = 100 —

a **Double 150** — [ ] — [ ]
— [ ] —

b **Double 350** — [ ] — [ ]
— [ ] —

2 A restaurant sells regular and double-sized portions.

a Complete the table to show the different amounts.

Some are in grams (g), some are in millilitres (ml), so remember to use the correct unit of measurement in your answer.

Number

Food / drink	Regular size	Double size
Fries	100 g	
Lemonade	350 ml	
Ice cream		300 g
Lamb curry and rice	400 g	

b Look at the double-size column. What do you notice?
Complete the sentence.
When a multiple of 50 is doubled, _____

_____

3 Multiples of 5 show the same pattern as multiples of 50 when you double them. Complete these number facts.

Multiples of 5:

Double 25 = ☐ Double 35 = ☐ Double 45 = ☐

Multiples of 50:

Double 250 = ☐ Double 350 = ☐ Double 450 = ☐

 1 a In this grid, there are pairs of numbers where one is double the other. Find each pair and colour them the same colour.

b What letter of the alphabet have you shaded? ☐

150	65	600	16	2
45	500	130	400	15
100	25	19	9	85
21	350	8	450	22
300	300	38	7	5

143

Number

Lesson 4: **Multiplying single-digit numbers by 2, 3, 4, 5, 6, 9 and 10 (3)**

- Multiply a single-digit number by 2, 3, 4, 5, 6, 9 or 10

You will need
- coloured pencils

Challenge 1

1 a Draw 4 groups of 6.

How many altogether? ☐

b Draw 3 groups of 9.

How many altogether? ☐

2 Complete these multiplication calculations.

a ●●●
●●● 2 × 3 = ☐

b ●●●●●●
●●●●●● 6 × 2 = ☐

c ●●●●●●●●●●
●●●●●●●●●● 10 × 2 = ☐

Challenge 2

1 a There are five incorrect facts in this grid. Colour them.

×	2	6	9	10
4	8	24	34	40
7	16	42	62	70
3	12	16	27	30
5	10	30	45	50

b Write the five correct facts below.

☐ ☐

☐ ☐

☐

2 Write down each child's multiplication.

a

I multiplied
two odd single-digit
numbers together and
got the answer 27.

⬜ × ⬜ = ⬜

b

I multiplied
the same single-digit
numbers together and
got the answer 36.

⬜ × ⬜ = ⬜

c

I multiplied
a single-digit number
that is one more than the
other one and got the
answer 20.

⬜ × ⬜ = ⬜

d

I multiplied
two single-digit
numbers that are more
than 5 and got the
answer 54.

⬜ × ⬜ = ⬜

Challenge 3

Each of these strategies is a way of working out the answer to a single-digit number multiplied by 2, 3, 4, 5, 6, 9 or 10.

Draw a line to match each strategy with the correct multiplication.

a Double the first number, then double it again. •

• 8 × 9

b Multiply the first number by 10, then subtract one of that number. •

• 7 × 4

c Multiply the second number by 5, then add another one more of that number. •

• 9 × 6

d Multiply the first number by 3 and then double the answer. •

• 6 × 5

Lesson 5: **Multiplying teens numbers by 3 and 5 (1)**

Number

• Multiply a teens numbers by 3 and 5

Challenge 1 Show how each number can be partitioned into tens and units.

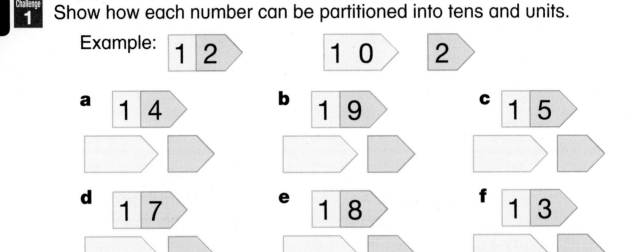

Example: 1 2 → 1 0 → 2

a 1 4 →

b 1 9 →

c 1 5 →

d 1 7 →

e 1 8 →

f 1 3 →

Challenge 2

1 Partition each of these teens numbers to help multiply them by 3 or 5.

Example:

$14 \times 3 = \boxed{10 \times 3} + \boxed{4 \times 3}$

$= \boxed{30 + 12}$

$= \boxed{42}$

a $13 \times 3 = \boxed{} + \boxed{}$

$= \boxed{}$

$= \boxed{}$

b $15 \times 3 = \boxed{} + \boxed{}$

$= \boxed{}$

$= \boxed{}$

c $16 \times 5 = \boxed{} + \boxed{}$

$= \boxed{}$

$= \boxed{}$

d $17 \times 5 = \boxed{} + \boxed{}$

$= \boxed{}$

$= \boxed{}$

Number

2 Use the box to show your working out for each question.

a Bryony reads 5 pages of her book every day. How many pages will she read in 2 weeks?

☐ pages

b Football teams get 3 points each time they win. How many points will a team have if they play 16 games and win them all?

☐ points

Challenge 3 Amira spins a spinner 4 times. She gets the digits 1, 6, 4 and 5.

She uses the digits to make a teens number multiplied by a single-digit.

a What is the largest total Amira can make?

The largest multiplication is 1☐ × ☐ = ☐

b What is the smallest total Amira can make?

The smallest multiplication is 1☐ × ☐ = ☐

☹ 😐 ☺

Number

Lesson 6: **Multiplying teens numbers by 3 and 5 (2)**

• Multiply a teen numbers by 3 and 5

Challenge 1

For each number, show how it can be partitioned into tens and units.

a   13 can be split into ⟨10⟩ and ⟨3⟩.

b   16 can be split into ☐ and ☐.

c   18 can be split into ☐ and ☐.

d   15 can be split into ☐ and ☐.

e   14 can be split into ☐ and ☐.

Challenge 2

1   Partition each teens number to help multiply by 3 or 5.

Example:

13×5
- $10 \times 5 = 50$
- $3 \times 5 = 15$
- $50 + 15 = 65$

a 16×3

b 18×5

c 18×3

2 a Sam's mum gives him 5 portions of fruit and vegetables to eat every day. How many portions will he eat in 17 days?

[   ] portions

b Sam's mum also encourages him to brush his teeth 3 times a day. How many times will he brush his teeth in 19 days?

[   ] times

Challenge 3 Jayden multiplies a teens number by 4 and gets the answer 68.

Olivia thinks she knows what the calculation was because she sees the 8 digit on the end. She uses it to think of multiples of 4 that make numbers that end in an 8.

Yusuf thinks he knows what the calculation was because he knows that ten 4s make 40. He uses this to help.

Kaya tries lots of different teens numbers until she makes the answer 68.

Use one of these methods (or any other strategy) to help you work out what Jayden's multiplication was.

Jayden's calculation was [   ] × 4 = 68

149

Number

Lesson 7: **Dividing 2-digit numbers by 2, 3, 4, 5, 6, 9 and 10 (3)**

• Divide a 2-digit number by 2, 3, 4, 5, 6, 9 or 10

Count the jumps backwards from each number to help answer the questions.

a

3 6 9 12 15 18 21 24 27 30

How many 3s in 27? ☐   How many 3s in 18? ☐

How many 3s in 30? ☐   How many 3s in 12? ☐

b

6 12 18 24 30 36 42 48 54 60

How many 6s in 24? ☐   How many 6s in 36? ☐

How many 6s in 48? ☐   How many 6s in 54? ☐

1 The table shows the numbers of children who take part in different sports at a school.

If there are 20 children in Class 3:

a How many lacrosse teams can they split themselves into? ☐

b How many relay teams can they split themselves into? ☐

c How many 5-a-side football teams can they split themselves into ☐

Sport / Activity	Number of children taking part
gymnastics	3 per group
relay race	4 per team
5-a-side football	5 per team
ice hockey	6 per team
baseball	9 per team
lacrosse	10 per team

Number

2 Fill in the answers.

a $81 \div 9 = \boxed{}$ **b** $42 \div 6 = \boxed{}$

c $40 \div 5 = \boxed{}$ **d** $18 \div 3 = \boxed{}$

e $10 \div 2 = \boxed{}$ **f** $90 \div 10 = \boxed{}$

g $12 \div 4 = \boxed{}$ **h** $27 \div 9 = \boxed{}$

i $12 \div 6 = \boxed{}$ **j** $18 \div 2 = \boxed{}$

 Challenge 3

1 Class 2 split into teams of 4 to practise relay races. There is 1 child left over. How many children could be in the class altogether? $\boxed{}$ children

2 Class 1 split into teams of 5 to play a game of 5-a-side football. There are 3 children left over. How many children could be in the class altogether? $\boxed{}$ children

3 Can you think of a class size where they can all play baseball, ice hockey or do gymnastics?

☹ 😐 ☺

151

Lesson 8: **Dividing 2-digit numbers by 2, 3, 4, 5, 6, 9 and 10 (4)**

- Divide a 2-digit number by 2, 3, 4, 5, 6, 9 or 10

You will need
- coloured pencils

 1 Share 15 cubes equally into 5 groups. Draw the groups.

How many cubes are in each group? ☐

2 Share 18 cubes equally into 9 groups. Draw the groups.

How many cubes are in each group? ☐

 1 Divide these numbers by counting in multiples and see how many fit into the number. Use the blank number lines to show your working.

Example: 78 ÷ 6 = 13

0   60   66   72   78

a 85 ÷ 5 = ☐

b 130 ÷ 10 = ☐

c $60 \div 3 = \boxed{}$

2 Some of these division calculations have a remainder. For example: 49 ÷ 4 has a remainder of 1 because twelve 4s are 48.

Colour in the division calculations that do **not** have a remainder.

41 ÷ 3	28 ÷ 2	142 ÷ 10	95 ÷ 5
68 ÷ 6	180 ÷ 10	35 ÷ 2	45 ÷ 3
87 ÷ 5	102 ÷ 9	108 ÷ 9	52 ÷ 4

 Challenge 3

1 Two is half of four. There are eighteen 2s in a mystery number. Estimate how many 4s you think there will be.

My estimate: $\boxed{}$

The mystery number is $\boxed{}$. Now work out the actual number of 4s.

$\boxed{} \div 4 = \boxed{}$

2 Three is half of six. There are thirty-four 3s in a mystery number. Estimate how many 6s you think there will be.

My estimate: $\boxed{}$

The mystery number is $\boxed{}$. Now work out the actual number of 6s.

$\boxed{} \div 6 = \boxed{}$

Geometry

Lesson 1: **Identifying and describing 2D shapes**

• Identify 2D shapes according to their properties

 1 Label these shapes. Choose the names from the box.

triangle	irregular pentagon	regular pentagon
rectangle	regular hexagon	irregular hexagon
	regular octagon	semi-circle

_____ _____ _____ _____

_____ _____ _____

2 What 2D shapes can you see in this picture?

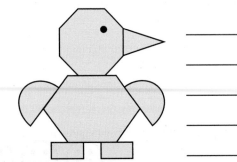

_____

_____

_____

_____

_____

1 a Draw a shape picture using different shapes. Colour each shape a different colour.

b Write the names of the shapes you used.

_____

2 Look at the shapes.

  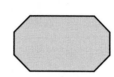

a Circle a regular shape and describe its properties.

_____

b Circle an irregular shape and describe its properties.

_____

1 a Draw a line to split this octagon into a right-angled hexagon.

b Put a cross next to the right angles you have made in your hexagon.

c How do you know the shape is a hexagon?

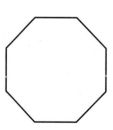

_____

2 Write a definition of a vertex.

_____

_____

Geometry

Lesson 2: **Drawing 2D shapes**

• Recognise 2D shapes in drawings

Challenge 1 Draw lines to complete these shapes.

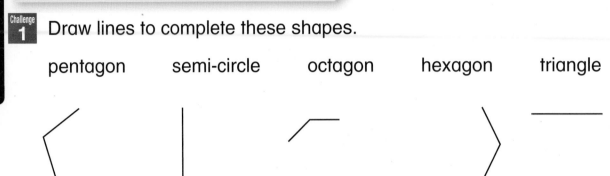

pentagon   semi-circle   octagon   hexagon   triangle

Challenge 2

1 Draw a semi-circle and describe its properties.
Include these words:

curved   straight   side   symmetry   right angles

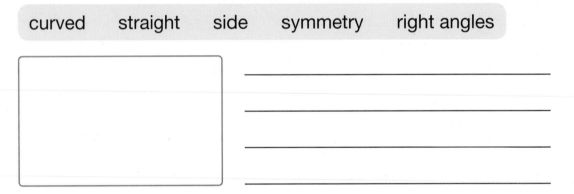

2 a Label these regular shapes.

_____   _____   _____   _____

b Draw an irregular shape for each of the shapes above.

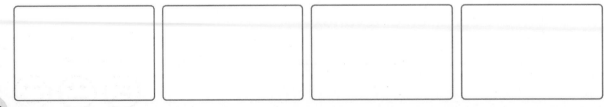

Challenge 3

1 Draw a hexagon with 2 right angles.

2 Draw an octagon with 3 right angles.

Geometry

157

Geometry

Lesson 3: **2D shapes and right angles**

- Identify 2D shapes and right angles in the environment

Challenge 1 Tick the right angles.

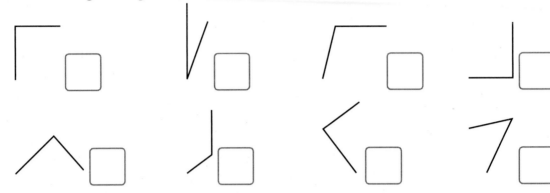

Challenge 2 **1** Circle the right angles in these pictures.

2 a What size of turn is a right angle?

_____

b What size of turn is 2 right angles?

_____

c What size of turn is 4 right angles?

_____

1 Use this shape as the centre shape for a tiling pattern.

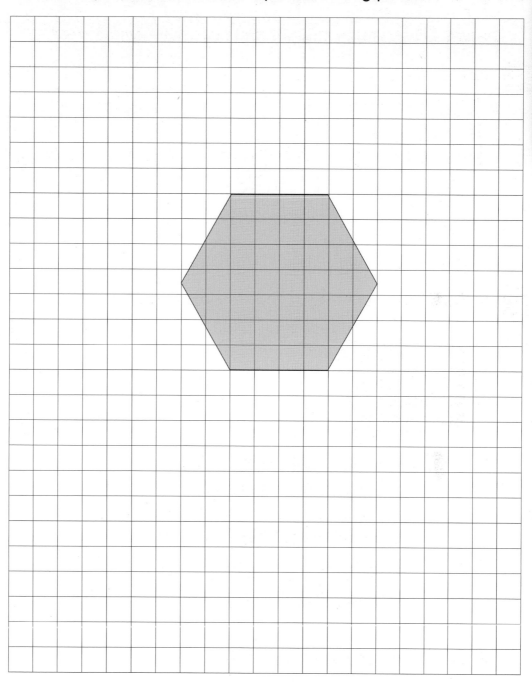

2 What other 2D shapes did you use?

_____

_____

Lesson 4: **2D shapes and symmetry**

• Identify symmetry in shapes and the environment

Geometry

Challenge 1 Draw one line of symmetry on each of these shapes.

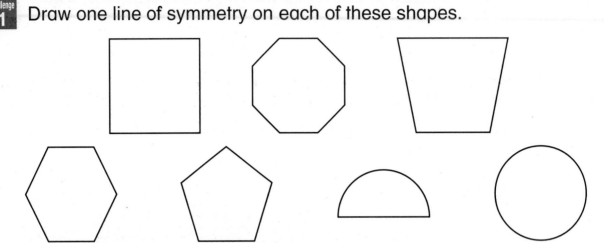

Challenge 2 **1** Draw two lines of symmetry on each of these shapes

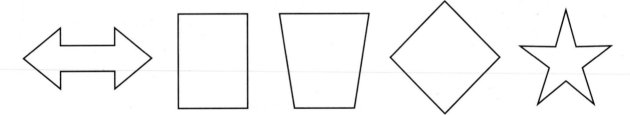

2 What is symmetry?

_____

_____

_____

3 Draw all the lines of symmetry on these shapes.

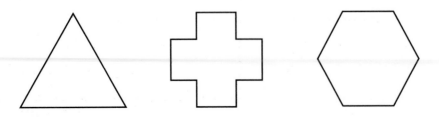

1 Complete this pattern so that it is symmetrical.

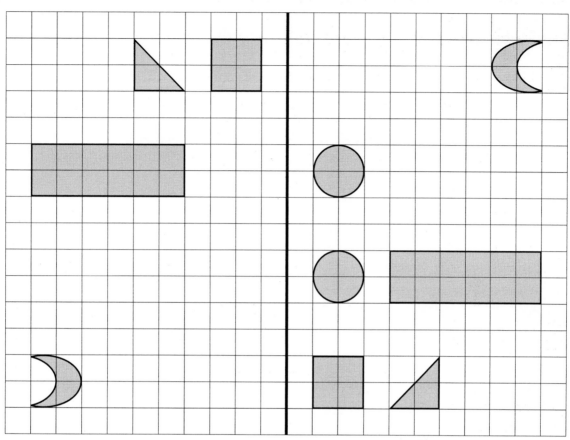

line of symmetry

2 Now make your own symmetrical pattern on this grid.

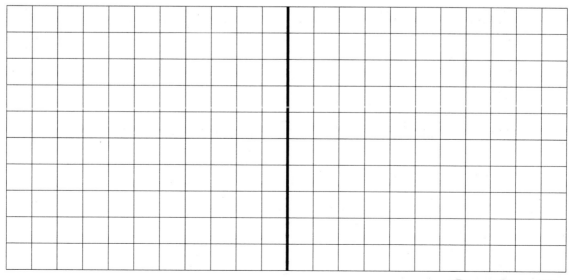

Lesson 1: **Identifying 3D shapes**

• Identify, describe and classify 3D shapes

 Draw lines to match each 3D shape with its name.
Choose the names from the box.

| sphere | square-based pyramid | cylinder | cuboid | cone | cube |

 1 What are the properties of a square-based pyramid?

_____

_____

2 Use the properties of the shapes to complete the Carroll diagram.

sphere   square-based   cube   cuboid
                    pyramid

cylinder   cone   triangular-based
                                                  pyramid

	square faces	no square faces
12 edges		
not 12 edges		

Challenge 3

1 Look at the Carroll diagram in Challenge 2.

a Which section is empty?

_____

b Why do you think this is?

_____

_____

2 a Copy this shape onto some squared paper. Cut it out and fold along the dashed lines.

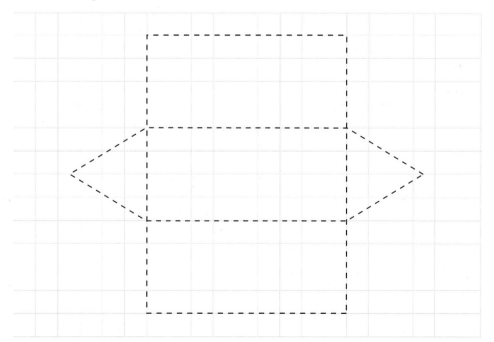

b What 3D shape can you make from this net?

_____

163

Geometry

Lesson 2: **Making 3D shapes**

• Identify and make 3D shapes

Challenge 1 Tick the shapes that are prisms, then name them.

 ☐

 ☐

_____   _____

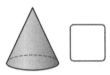 ☐

 ☐

_____   _____

Challenge 2 Draw lines to match the 3D shapes to the name labels.

cone

sphere

rectangular prism

cube

cylinder

cylinder

Challenge 3

1 Copy these shapes onto some squared paper. Cut them out and fold along the dashed lines.

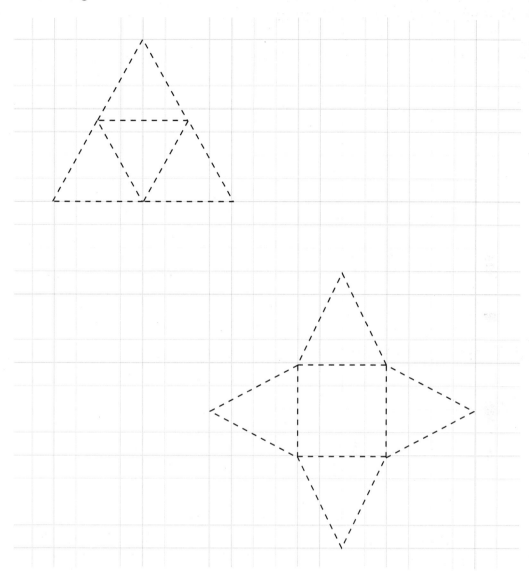

2 What 3D shapes can you make from these nets?

_____

_____

_____

Geometry

Lesson 3: **Nets of a cube**

• Draw a net for a cube and make a cube

1 Tick the shapes which are cubes.

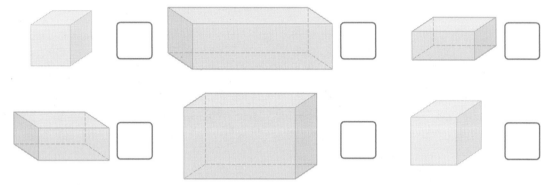

2 Complete the table to show the properties of a cube.

Number of faces	
Number of vertices	
Number of edges	
Is it a prism?	

Challenge 2

1 Describe how a cube is different from a cuboid.

_____

_____

2 Look closely at a cube. Now draw and label it.

3 Tick the nets which will make a cube.

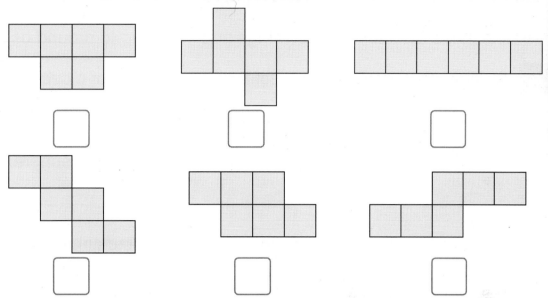

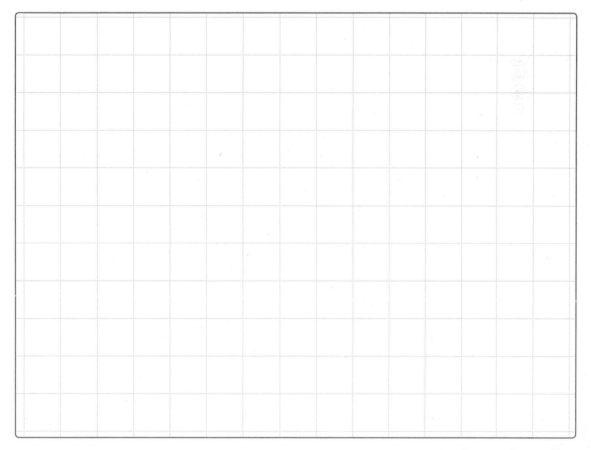

Challenge 3 There are 11 possible nets of a cube. Draw 2 more nets that have not yet been shown.

☹ 😐 ☺ 167

Geometry

Lesson 4: **Recognising 3D shapes**

• Recognise 3D shapes in drawings and in the world around us

Challenge 1

1 Write the name of an object that is the shape of a cube.

_____

2 Write the name of an object that is the shape of a sphere.

_____

3 Write where you would see cubes and cuboids in real life.

_____

_____

_____

Challenge 2

1 Write the names of the 3D shapes you can see in the picture.

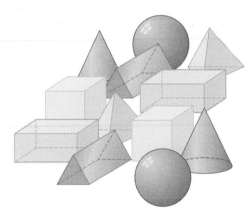

_____

_____

_____

2 Make a list of objects that you can see in the classroom and write the names of the 3D shapes that make them.

_____

_____

_____

_____

 Challenge 3

1 Use 3D shapes to build a real-life model of this shape.

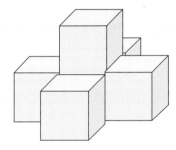

2 Draw the individual 3D shapes that make up the shape in the picture above.

3 Compare your answer to a partner's answer. Have you drawn the same 3D shapes? _____

☹ 😐 ☺

Geometry

Lesson 1: **Position, direction and movement (1)**

• Use the language of position and place objects in different positions

Challenge 1

1 Where is the cube?

_____

_____

2 Draw a triangle to the right of a square.

Challenge 2

1 Where is the cuboid? Describe its position in 3 different ways.

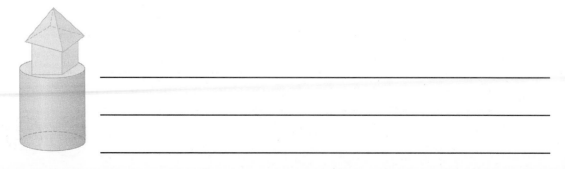

_____

_____

_____

2 Draw a circle, square and pentagon. The pentagon needs to be to the right of the square. The circle needs to be to the right of the pentagon.

3 a Where is the sphere?

_____

b Where is the cylinder?

_____

c Where is the square-based pyramid?

_____

Challenge 3 Draw your own picture with five 2D shapes. Describe where each shape is positioned, in as many ways as you can.

_____
_____
_____
_____

Lesson 2: **Position, direction and movement (2)**

• Describe movement and move in different directions

1 Tick the clockwise turns.

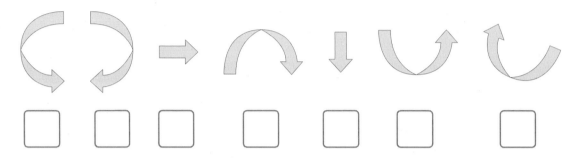

☐ ☐ ☐ ☐ ☐ ☐ ☐

2 Tick the anticlockwise turns.

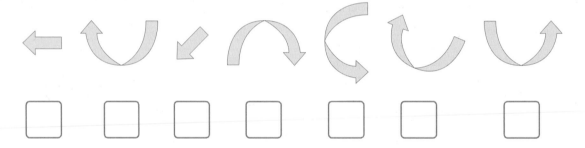

☐ ☐ ☐ ☐ ☐ ☐ ☐

1 Draw a cross in the top left square and then follow the instructions.

    a Draw a cross 4 squares to the right.

    b Draw a cross 3 squares below your last cross.

    c Draw a cross 2 squares to the left of your last cross.

    d Draw a cross 1 square above your last cross.

    e Draw a cross 2 squares to the left of your last cross.

    f Draw a cross 2 squares below your last cross.

2 Draw a road sign to show a left turn.

3 Draw a road sign to show a right turn.

Challenge 3

1 Draw 5 crosses on the grid. Join them with horizontal and vertical lines.

Use the words **left**, **right** and **up**, **down** to describe how to get from one cross to another.

_____

_____

_____

_____

_____

2 Write two sentences. Use the word **clockwise** in the first one and the word **anticlockwise** in the second.

_____

_____

_____

_____

Geometry

Lesson 3: **Square grids (1)**

• Find and describe a position on a grid

Challenge 1

1 Look at the grid. Put a tick beside the rows. Put a cross above the columns.

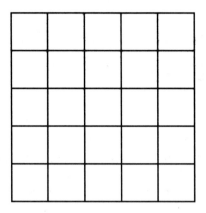

2 Colour these squares: AB, C1, D1 and B2.

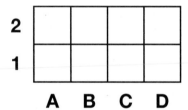

A   B   C   D

Challenge 2

1 Label the grid with numbers and letters.

Colour C2, D3, E4, C3, D4, E2, C4, D2 and E3.

What shape have you made?

_____

_____

2 Look at the objects in the grid. Using the letters and numbers, write down the position of each of them on the grid.

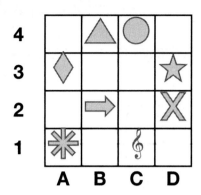
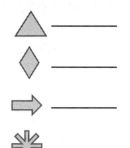
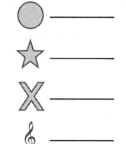

Challenge 3

1 Label this grid with numbers and letters.

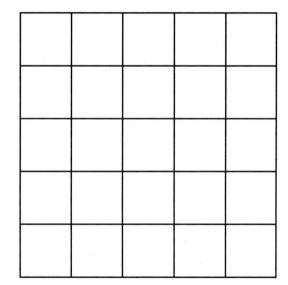

2 Colour squares A1, C5, E5, D2, A3, C3, A5, B4, D4.

3 Which other squares do you need to colour to complete the pattern?

_____

_____

Geometry

Lesson 4: **Square grids (2)**

• Find and describe a position on a grid

You will need
• coloured pencils

Challenge 1 Write the positions of the pentagons on the grid.

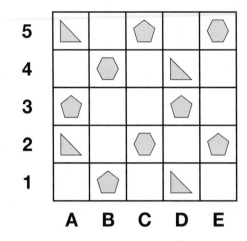

_____

_____

_____

Challenge 2

1 Colour the squares C3, E2, B5, A1 and D4.

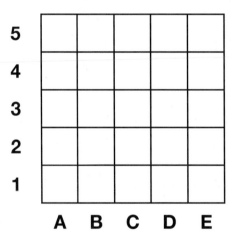

2 Your friend wants to move a counter from square A1 to square B5, going through the other squares you have shaded. Write directions for this route, using the correct direction words you have learned.

_____

_____

_____

_____

Challenge 3 Colour 12 squares to make a symmetrical pattern.

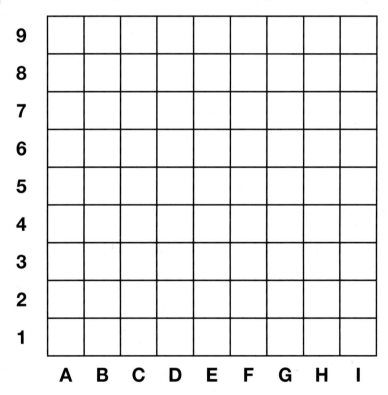

Which squares did you colour?

_____

_____

177

Lesson 5: **Drawing right angles**

Geometry

• Use a set square to draw right angles

Challenge 1 **1**

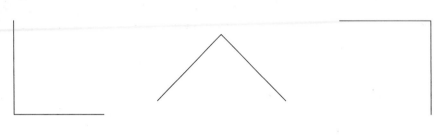

    a What is the same about these lines?

_____

_____

    b What is different about these lines?

_____

_____

2 Complete the 2D shape that you can make from these right angles.

Challenge 2 **1** Tick the two right angles that have been made by this group of shapes.

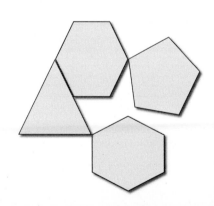

2 Use your set square to draw an accurate:

a square

b rectangle.

Geometry

1 Use a set square to draw a hexagon with three right angles.

2 Use a set square to draw an octagon with four right angles.

Lesson 6: **Comparing angles**

Geometry

• Compare angles with right angles

You will need
• set square
• ruler

Challenge 1

1 Tick the angles that are smaller than a right angle.

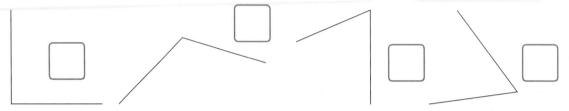

2 Tick the angles that are larger than a right angle.

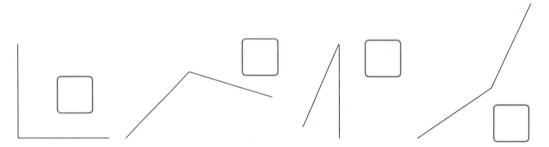

Challenge 2

1 Tick the angles in this picture that are smaller than a right angle.

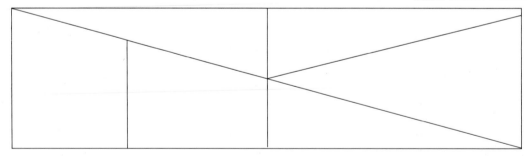

2 Tick the angles in this picture that are larger than a right angle.

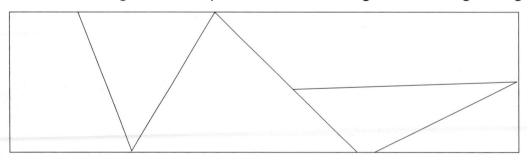

3 a Draw a 4-sided shape that has two angles that are larger than a right angle.

b Describe the size of the other two angles.

_____

Challenge 3

1 a Draw a 5-sided shape.

b Describe the size of the angles.

_____

2 a What is the name of an angle that is smaller than a right angle?

_____

b What is the name of an angle that is larger than a right angle?

_____

Geometry

Lesson 7: **Right angles and straight lines**

• Compare right angles with straight lines

You will need

• red and blue coloured pencil

Challenge 1

1 Tick the straight lines.

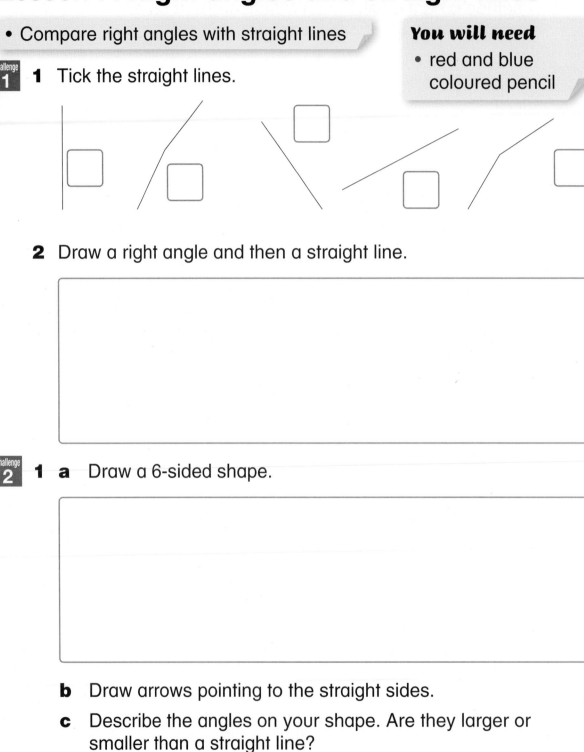

2 Draw a right angle and then a straight line.

Challenge 2

1 a Draw a 6-sided shape.

b Draw arrows pointing to the straight sides.

c Describe the angles on your shape. Are they larger or smaller than a straight line?

2 Tick the angles that are larger than a right angle in red and the angles that are smaller than a right angle in blue.

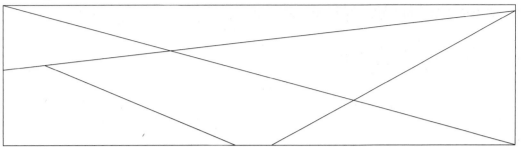

 1 Describe a straight line angle.

_____

_____

2 If you turn one of these lines about the point where they meet, you could make a straight line. What sort of angle would you turn the line through?

_____

Use drawings to explain why.

183

Geometry

Lesson 8: **Angles are everywhere**

• Recognise angles in the world around us

 1 Order these angles, from smallest to largest.

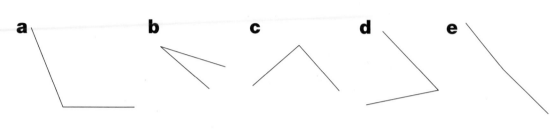

a   b   c   d   e

_____

2 Draw the following angles.

right angle	straight line

obtuse angle	acute angle

 1 Look at this shape.

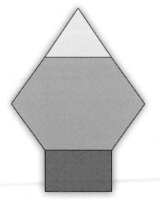

a How many right angles can you see? ☐

b How many angles that are smaller than a right angle can you see? ☐

c How many angles that are larger that a right angle can you see? ☐

d How many straight line angles can you see? ☐

2 What angles and lines can you see in this picture of an office? Draw arrows and label the different angles and lines. One has been done for you.

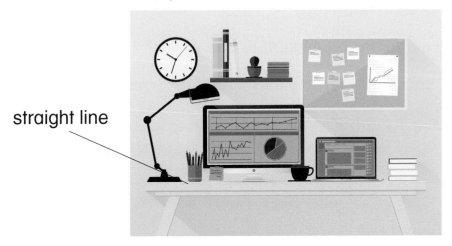

straight line

Challenge 3

1 Visualise a square. Cut it in half diagonally. Draw the shape you have now.

What types of angles does your new shape have?

_____

_____

_____

2 Think about a square. Now imagine cutting off one corner. Draw and name the shape that is left.

Lesson 1: **Notes and coins**

* Write money in the correct way

Measure

1 How many cents are equivalent to one dollar?

2 How much money is here? Write the total correctly.

1 How much money is here? Write the total correctly.

2 a Libby had $5 in notes and 132 cents. How much money did she have altogether?
Write the total correctly.

b What is the smallest number of notes and coins that could make up this total?

Measure

1 What notes and coins could you use to pay for each of these items? Write at least three different combinations of notes and coins for each item.

a

b

c

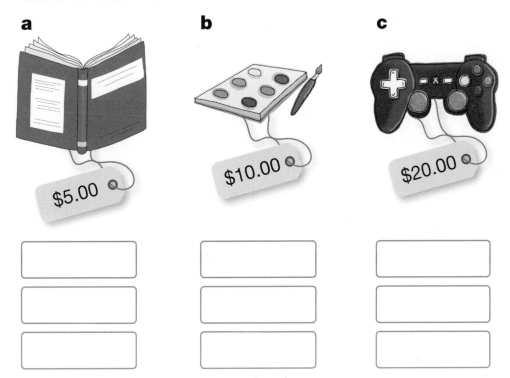

$5.00

$10.00

$20.00

2 a How much is in each pile?

b What is the difference in value between the two piles?

187

Lesson 2: **Finding totals**

- Find totals of amounts of money

Challenge 1

Rasheed bought 2 racing cars.
They each cost $7.75.
How much did he spend?

Show how you worked out
your answer in the box.

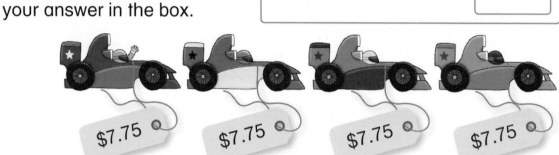

Challenge 2

1 a India bought an apple, a banana and a pear. How much did
she spend? Show how you worked this out in the box.

b Draw the fewest notes and coins that India could have used
to pay for her fruit.

2 a Yukesh bought 2 oranges and a banana. How much did he spend?

_____

b Show how you worked this out in the box.

c Draw the fewest notes and coins that Yukesh could have used to pay for his fruit.

Challenge 3

1 a Look at the price list in Challenge 2.

Ranjir bought 2 of each fruit. How much did he spend?

_____

b Show how you worked this out in the box.

2 Use the price list to make up, and solve, your own number problem.

_____

_____

☹ 😐 ☺

189

Measure

Lesson 3: **Giving change**

* Find the coins and notes to make totals and give change

You will need
* selection of notes and coins

Challenge 1

1 a Anji spent $1.25 on some stickers and 85c on a pen.

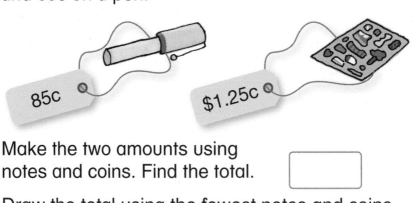

85c

$1.25c

Make the two amounts using notes and coins. Find the total.

b Draw the total using the fewest notes and coins.

2 a Anji bought one set of stickers and gave the seller $2. How much change did she receive?

b Show how you worked this out in the box below.

Challenge 2

1 a Samir had $20. He bought a racing car. How much change did he get?

$19.35　　$17.75　　$8.90　　$7.45　　$3.50

b Show how you worked out your answer.

2 Pierre bought a remote control car with a $50 note.

How much change did he get?

Challenge 3

1 a Ibrahim had saved $25. He spent $14.15 on a chess set. How much money did he have left?

b Show how you worked out your answer.

2 Dalia had $20. She wanted to buy a doll for $12.80 and a game for $7.40.

a Does she have enough money?

b Explain your answer.

Measure

Lesson 4: **Solving problems with money**

• Solve money problems by using multiplication and division

Challenge 1

1 a Ranvir bought 3 kg of potatoes.
Each kilogram costs $2.50.

How much did she spend? ☐

b Ranvir also bought $\frac{1}{2}$ kg of bananas.
Each kilogram costs $4.50.

How much did she
spend on bananas? ☐

Potatoes

$2.50 $4.50

c Show how you worked this out.

☐

Challenge 2

Cinema tickets cost $4.80 each. Children's tickets are
half price.

$4.80

a How much would it cost a family of 2 adults and 3 children?
Show your working out in the box.

☐

b How much would it cost 5 children and 1 adult? Show your
working out in the box.

☐

Measure

c Popcorn costs $1.90 for a small carton. A large carton is double this amount.

A group of 7 children and 3 adults each buy a cinema ticket. The group also buy 6 small cartons of popcorn and 1 large carton. How much does the group spend in total? Show your working out in the box.

$1.90

Challenge 3 A return train ticket costs $15. A one-way ticket costs half this amount. A child's ticket costs half the price of a full ticket.

a 2 adults buy return tickets and 1 adult buys a one-way ticket. What is the total cost? Show your working out in the box.

b 3 adults buy return tickets, 1 adult buys a one-way ticket and 5 one-way tickets for his children. What is the total cost? Show your working out in the box.

c A family of 5 buy two adult returns tickets and 3 child return tickets. They pay with a $100 note. How much change will they get? Show your working out in the box.

193

Measure

Lesson 1: **Estimating, measuring and recording length**

• Choose and use units and equipment to measure length

You will need
• metre stick
• ruler

1 Tick the things that you would measure in centimetres.

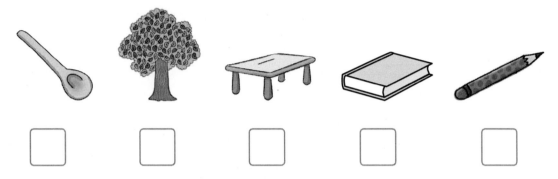

☐ ☐ ☐ ☐ ☐

2 Write a list of six objects in the classroom that you would measure in centimetres.

_____   _____

_____   _____

_____   _____

1 Write the names of four different pieces of equipment that you could use to measure length.

_____   _____

_____   _____

2 Find four objects in the classroom. Fill in the table by writing the unit you would use to measure the length of each object. Then, estimate the measurement before taking the actual measurement. Finally, include the equipment you use to take your measurement.

Name of object	Unit of measurement	Estimated measurement	Actual measurement	Equipment used to measure

Challenge 3

1 Take a metre stick and a ruler. Find three objects that you estimate are longer than the metre stick and three that you estimate are shorter than the ruler. Write the objects below, along with your estimates and the actual measurements.

	Name of object	Estimated measurement	Actual measurement
Longer than the metre stick			
Shorter than the ruler			

2 Write three examples of things you would measure in kilometres.

_____

_____

3 Write a sentence to describe what is meant by **length**.

_____

_____

Measure

Lesson 2: **Units of length**

- Convert between centimetres and metres, and metres and kilometres

Challenge 1

1 How many centimetres are there in 4 m? ☐ cm

Show how you worked out your answer.

☐

2 How many metres are there in 2 km? ☐ m

Show how you worked out your answer.

☐

Challenge 2

1 Order these lengths, from shortest to longest.

10 km   5 cm   12 m   3 km   25 cm   41 m

_____

2 Look at a metre stick. How many 10 cm lengths would be the same as 1 m? ☐

3 Look at a ruler. How many would you need to create a length a little longer than 1 m? ☐

Measure

4 Write eight facts from 5 m = 500 cm.

Explain the strategies you used to work these out.

Challenge 3

1 a Dana wondered what length she would have if she converted 3 km and 3 m to metres. What do you think? Show your answer and how you worked it out.

[ ] m

b How many centimetres would that be? [ ] cm

2 Write eight facts from $4\frac{1}{2}$ m = 450 cm. Be creative!

Explain your strategies for working these out.

197

Lesson 3: **Using a ruler**

Measure

- Draw and measure lines to the nearest centimetre with a ruler

You will need
- ruler

Challenge 1

1 Use your ruler to measure the lines. Write each measurement in centimetres.

_____ ⬚ cm

_____ ⬚ cm

_____ ⬚ cm

____ ⬚ cm

_____ ⬚ cm

2 Use your ruler to draw a line 11 cm long.

3 Use your ruler to draw a line 8 cm long.

Challenge 2

1 Saul drew a line. It was 6 cm long.

a Use your ruler to draw a line half the length of Saul's line.

b Use your ruler to draw a line twice the length of Saul's line.

2 a Measure the lines. Write the length of each one rounded to the nearest centimetre.

_____

[ ] cm

_____

[ ] cm

_____

[ ] cm

_____

[ ] cm

_____

[ ] cm

Measure

b Add the lengths of all five lines together.

What is the total length of all the lines?

[   ]

Challenge 3

1 Without using a ruler, draw six lines of different lengths on strips of paper. Now, cut the papers to the length of your lines. Label each strip from A (shortest) to F (longest). Estimate the length of each one. Measure them.

Work out the difference between your estimate and the actual length. Complete the table.

Strip	Estimate	Actual	Difference
A			
B			
C			
D			
E			
F			

2 Write instructions to tell someone how to use a ruler to measure the length of a line.

_____

_____

Measure

Lesson 4: **Solving problems involving length**

• Solve word problems involving length

Challenge 1

1 a Dan drew a square. One side was 6 cm. Draw Dan's square.

b What is the total length of the sides of his square? How did you work this out?

_____

_____

_____

Challenge 2

1 Caira had 10 ribbons. Each one measured 15 cm. What was the total length of all her ribbons? Write your answer in centimetres, and then metres and centimetres.

[   ] cm   [   ] m [   ] cm

Show how you worked out your answer.

2 Sami sprinted for 150 m. Paulo sprinted 3 times as far.

How far did Paulo sprint? [ ]

Show how you worked out your answer.

Challenge 3

1 Anhil measured the width of his vegetable garden. It was 3 times the width of Raheed's garden. Raheed's was 2 m 50 cm. How wide was Anhil's garden?

[ ]

Show how you worked out your answer.

2 Make up, and solve, a word problem that includes these words:

farmer   seeds   field   distance

_____

_____

_____

_____

Lesson 1: **Estimating, measuring and recording mass**

Measure

- Choose and use units and equipment to measure mass

You will need
- 1 kg bag of rice
- 5 kg bag of potatoes

Challenge 1

1 a Tick the things you think have a mass of **less** than 1 kg.

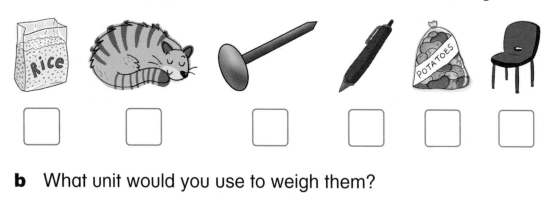

☐ ☐ ☐ ☐ ☐ ☐

b What unit would you use to weigh them?

_____

2 a Tick the things you think have a mass of **more** than 1 kg.

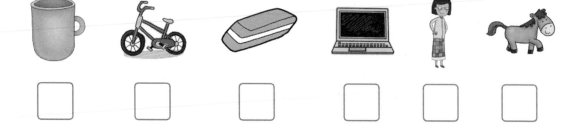

☐ ☐ ☐ ☐ ☐ ☐

b Why do you think these are measured in kilograms?

_____

Challenge 2

1 Write a list of six objects in the classroom that you would measure in kilograms.

_____   _____

_____   _____

_____   _____

2 Make a list of six objects that you would measure in grams.

_____   _____

_____   _____

_____   _____

3 Use the 1 kg bag of rice to help you estimate three objects in the classroom that weigh approximately 1 kg. Write the objects and your estimated mass of each one.

Object	Estimated mass

Challenge 3

1 Use the 5 kg bag of potatoes to help you estimate three objects that are between 4 kg and 5 kg. Write the objects and your estimated mass of each one.

Object	Estimated mass

2 a Write a sentence to describe what is meant by **mass**.

_____

_____

b What is meant by **weight**?

_____

_____

Measure

Lesson 2: **Units of mass**

> • Convert between grams and kilograms, and kilograms and grams

Challenge 1

1 Write how many grams are in:

   a 3 kg   **b** 10 kg   **c** 7 kg   **d** 9 kg

   ☐ g   ☐ g   ☐ g   ☐ g

2 Write how many kilograms are in:

   a 2500 g ☐ kg   **b** 6500 g ☐ kg

   c 3000 g ☐ kg   **d** 12,000 g ☐ kg

Challenge 2

1 a Order these masses, from heaviest to lightest.

    $\frac{1}{2}$ kg   800 g   2 kg   100 g   50 kg   50 g

_____

   b How many 100 g weights would be the same as 1 kg? ☐

   c How many 10 g weights would be the same as 1 kg? ☐

2 If you had these weights, what would be their total mass? ☐
Show how you worked out your answer.

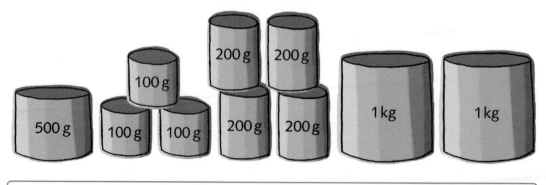

☐

Measure

3 Draw lines to match the equivalent weights.

10 kg	2000 g	500 g	$7\frac{1}{2}$ kg

7500 g	10 000 g	2 kg	$\frac{1}{2}$ kg

Challenge 3

1 What mass would Ciara have if she converted the total of 7 kg and 750 g, to grams? Give your answer, showing your working.

2 Write four possible ways to make 4 kg 250 g, using some or all of these weights.

Measure

Lesson 3: **Using scales**

- Read the mass of objects using scales

You will need
- set of scales
- modelling clay
- classroom objects

Challenge 1

1 Record the masses shown on the scales.

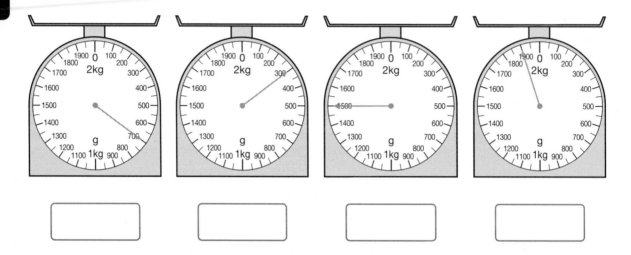

2 Draw the pointers on these scales to show:

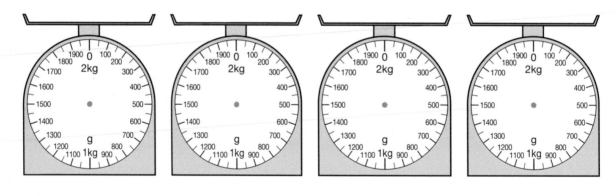

   a 200 g   **b** 700 g   **c** 1 kg 100 g   **d** 1 kg 800 g

Challenge 2

1 Samson weighed a piece of clay. It was 200 g. Use the scales and modelling clay to weigh an amount three times the mass of Saul's.

   a How much did it weigh?

   b Now weigh one half the mass. How much did it weigh?

Measure

2 Find four objects from the classroom. Weigh them to the nearest 100 g. Complete the table.

Object	Mass

3 Make four ball shapes from the modelling clay. Estimate their masses. Weigh them and complete the table.

Ball	Estimate	Actual	Difference
1			
2			
3			
4			

Challenge 3

Use the modelling clay to make three cubes. The second cube must be twice the mass of the first. The third must be twice the mass of the second.
Weigh them, then draw your cubes and their masses on these scales.

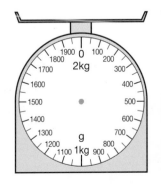  

Lesson 4: **Solving problems involving mass**

• Solve word problems involving mass

 Challenge 1

1 Ali bought 500 g of beans and 1 kg of potatoes. Draw the pointer on the scale to show the total mass of the beans and potatoes.

2 Dana bought 1 kg of rice, 250 g flour, 250 g lentils and 250 g sugar. Draw the pointer on the scale to show the total mass of the rice, flour, lentils and sugar.

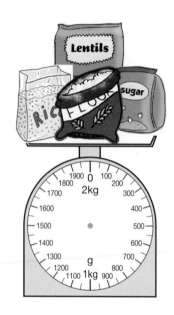

 Challenge 2

1 a Samson bought 3 kg 500 g of rice. Choose from the weights and draw those that will balance the pan scales.

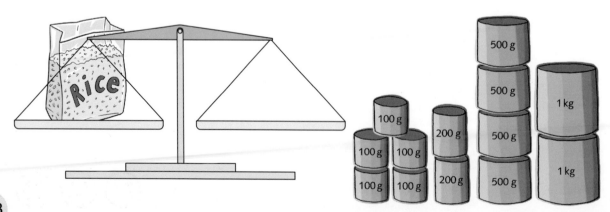

Measure

b What other combination of weights will balance the scales?

Draw your answer:

Challenge 3

1 Anita bought 1 kg 750 g of flour. Her friend bought twice as much. How much did her friend buy?

Show how you worked out your answer.

2 Yukesh and Samuel bought a total of 3 kg 500 g. Yukesh bought $\frac{1}{4}$ of the mass that Samuel bought.

What mass did they each buy?

Show how you worked out your answer.

209

Lesson 1: **Estimating, measuring and recording capacity**

Measure

• Choose and use units and equipment to measure capacity

Challenge 1

1 a Tick the things that you think have a capacity of **less** than 1 litre.

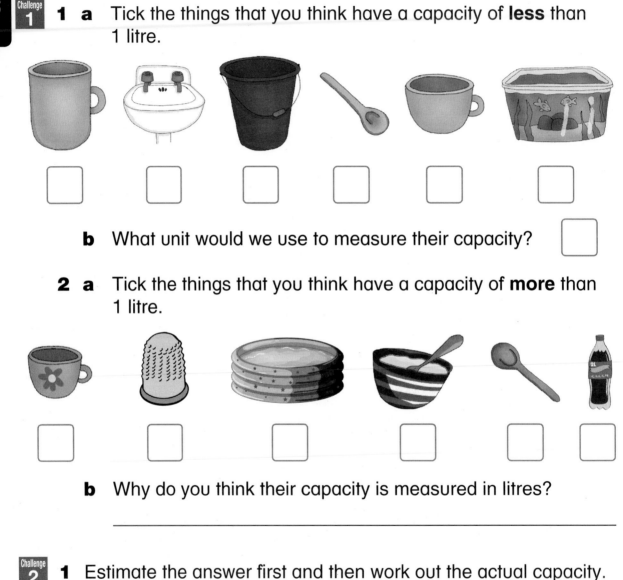

⬜ ⬜ ⬜ ⬜ ⬜ ⬜

b What unit would we use to measure their capacity? ⬜

2 a Tick the things that you think have a capacity of **more** than 1 litre.

⬜ ⬜ ⬜ ⬜ ⬜ ⬜

b Why do you think their capacity is measured in litres?

_____

Challenge 2

1 Estimate the answer first and then work out the actual capacity. Show your working.

a How many 500 ml jugs of water will it take to fill a 5 *l* bucket?

Estimate ⬜ Actual ⬜

b How many 5 *l* buckets of water will it take to fill an 80 *l* bath?

Estimate [   ] Actual [   ]

c How many times will you need to fill a 1 *l* jug to empty a 10 *l* barrel of water?

Estimate [   ] Actual [   ]

Challenge 3

1 Calculate the capacity. Remember to use the correct unit of measurement in your answer.

a 5 *l* = capacity of each = [   ]

b 1 *l* = capacity of each = [   ]

c 500 ml = capacity of each = [   ]

2 These measurements are in order, from smallest to largest. Cross out the measurements which are in the wrong place.

a 50 ml   100 ml   1 *l*   300 ml   750 ml   1 *l*   250 ml   3 *l*

b 7 *l*   12 *l*   25 *l*   30 ml   32 *l*   500 ml   38 *l*   100 *l*

☹ 😐 ☺

Unit **17** Capacity

Lesson 2: **Units of capacity**

Measure

• Convert between millilitres and litres, and litres and millilitres

Challenge 1

1 Write how many millilitres there are in:

    a 4 *l*   **b** 9 *l*   **c** 10 *l*   **d** 12 *l*

    [ ] ml   [ ] ml   [ ] ml   [ ] ml

2 Write how many litres there are in:

    a 6000 ml [ ] *l*   **b** 8500 ml [ ] *l*

    c 5000 ml [ ] *l*   **d** 10 000 ml [ ] *l*

Challenge 2

1 **a** Order these capacities, from greatest to least.

    3 *l*   900 ml $\frac{1}{4}$ *l*   400 ml $\frac{1}{2}$ *l*   1 *l*

    _____

    b How many 100 ml would be the same as 1 *l*? [ ] ml

    c How many 10 ml would be the same as 1 *l*? [ ] ml

2 Five containers have these capacities:

How much water would you need to fill them all? Show how you worked out your answer.

[ ]

3 Convert these measurements. Complete the table.

Millilitres	Litres
5800 ml	
	$7\frac{1}{2}l$
10 000 ml	
	$44l$

Explain the strategies you used to work these out.

_____

_____

_____

 Challenge 3

1 Sienna filled three jugs with juice. The smallest jug holds 500 ml. The second holds twice as much. The largest holds 4 times as much as the smallest. What is the total volume of juice? Show your working.

2 Make as many different totals as you can, using three of these amounts.

250ml   500ml   125ml   1 l

Measure

213

Measure

Lesson 3: **Using measuring vessels**

• Read capacity using the scale on measuring vessels

You will need

• water
• measuring vessel
• 4 cups

Draw the volume on each measuring cylinder to show:

a 300 ml   b 1 *l* 500 ml   c 850 ml   d 1 *l* 750 ml

| 2 *l* | 2 *l* | 2 *l* | 2 *l* |
| 1 *l* | 1 *l* | 1 *l* | 1 *l* |

1 Use water and a measuring vessel. Find the capacity of the four different cups that your teacher has given you. Write their capacities here:

☐ ☐ ☐ ☐

2 Pour different amounts of water into each cup. Now measure the volume of water in each, reading the scale on the measuring vessel. Complete the table.

Cup	Volume
1	
2	
3	
4	

214

Measure

3 Pour different amounts of water into each cup. Estimate the volume in each. Then measure the volume, using a measuring vessel. Compare your estimate with the actual volume. Complete the table.

Cup	Estimate	Actual	Difference
1			
2			
3			
4			

Challenge 3 Sharma was making up some juice for a picnic. She used 300 ml of apple concentrate and 1200 ml of water. Draw a measuring cylinder. Draw in the scale on the cylinder and show the total amount of juice that Sharma made.

Measure

Lesson 4: **Solving problems involving capacity**

• Solve word problems involving capacity

• coloured pencils

1 Raj poured 250 ml of apple juice into a measuring jug and added 1 *l* 500 ml of lemonade. Fill in the measuring jug to show how much drink he made.

2 Sue poured 750 ml of apple juice into a jug, adding 750 ml of lemonade. Fill in the measuring jug to show how much drink she made.

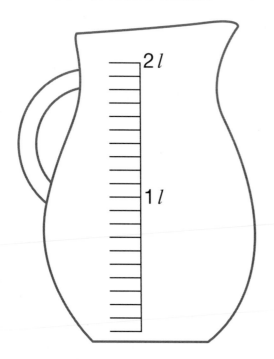

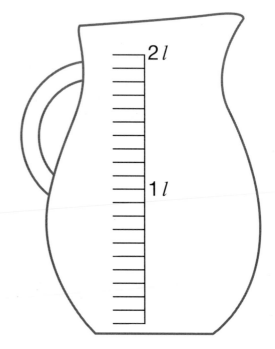

1 Four cups have these capacities.

  a 200 ml   **b** 750 ml   **c** 1 *l*   **d** 1 *l* 250 ml

Write the capacity of each cup if it was 3 times as much.

Write the capacity of each cup if it was half as much.

2 Simeon measured 250 ml of water into a glass. He measured 3 times as much into a second glass. He measured 4 times as much into a third glass. How much water did he use?

Show how you worked out your answer.

Challenge 3

1 Sara and Carmel bought a total of 4 l 800 ml of cola. Sara bought 3 times as much as Carmel. How much did they each buy? Show how you worked out your answer.

2 Make up and solve a word problem that includes these words:

milk   750 ml   2 people   café

Lesson 1: **Units of time**

Measure

* Choose and use units to measure time

You will need
* stopwatch
* interlocking cubes

Challenge 1

1 Write how many seconds are equivalent to:

a 2 minutes ☐ seconds **b** 5 minutes ☐ seconds

c 10 minutes ☐ seconds **d** 15 minutes ☐ seconds

2 Tick the analogue clocks.

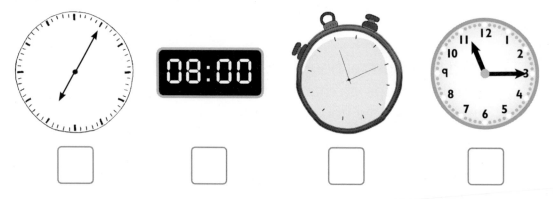

☐ ☐ ☐ ☐

Challenge 2

1 Write how many hours are equivalent to:

a 60 minutes ☐ hours **b** 300 minutes ☐ hours

c 120 minutes ☐ hours **d** 180 minutes ☐ hours

e 600 minutes ☐ hours **f** 360 minutes ☐ hours

2 Order these times, from shortest to longest.

120 minutes   120 seconds   1 hour   48 hours   1 day

_____

3 Work with a partner. You need a stopwatch and some interlocking cubes.

Ask your partner to time you for 1 minute.

How many cubes can you link together in 1 minute? ☐

218

4 Work out these time equivalences.

a How many days are there in a week?

b How many hours are in 1 day?

c How many minutes are in 1 hour?

d How many seconds are in 1 minute?

e How many seconds are in 10 minutes?

Measure

Challenge 3

1 Work with a partner. You need a stopwatch and some interlocking cubes.

Ask your partner to time you.

How many cubes can you link together in 30 seconds?

Now, together, work out how many cubes you could link together in:

a 1 minute

b 5 minutes

c $\frac{1}{4}$ of an hour

d half an hour

e 1 hour

f 1 day

2 a Describe an analogue clock.

_____

b Describe a digital clock.

_____

c How are analogue and digital clocks the same?

_____

d How are they different?

_____

219

Lesson 2: **Telling the time**

* Tell the time on analogue and digital clocks

Challenge 1

1 Draw the times on the clock faces.

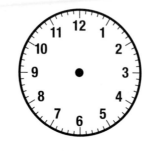

a 6 o'clock

b half past 10

c 20 minutes past 9

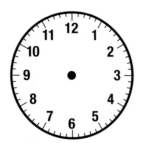

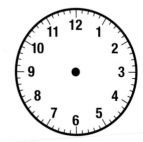

d 45 minutes past 2

e 35 minutes past 3

f $\frac{1}{4}$ past 11

2 Write the digital equivalent for these times.

a [:]

b [:]

c [:]

1 Draw the times on the analogue clocks.

a 2:30 **b** 10:45 **c** 8:05 **d** 12:35

2 Write the digital equivalent for these times.

a [:] **b** [:] **c** [:] **d** [:]

Challenge 3 This clock shows 50 minutes past 5 and 5:50. We can also read this time as 10 minutes to 6.

What are the 3 ways that we can read these times?

a  **b**  **c**

_____

_____

_____

☹ 😐 ☺

221

Measure

Lesson 3: **Calculating time intervals**

• Calculate time intervals in hours and minutes

You will need

• clock with moveable hands

Challenge 1

1 Use your clock to work out the time intervals.

a 2 o'clock to 3 o'clock

b 30 minutes past 3 to 4 o'clock

c 45 minutes past 6 to 7 o'clock

d 15 minutes past 1 to 2 o'clock

2 Write four times that have a time interval of 2 hours:

a

b

c

d

Challenge 2

1 India spent 1 hour and 40 minutes doing her homework.
She began at 3:55. What time did she finish?

Draw a time number line to work out your answer.

2 Ishmael finished his homework at 7:15. It took him 1 hour and 15 minutes. When did he start his homework?

Draw a time number line to work out your answer.

Measure

3 Samuel played a football game for 1 hour and 45 minutes.
The game started at 3 o'clock. When did it finish?

☐ : ☐

Yukesh left half an hour before the end.
When did he leave?

☐ : ☐

Draw a time number line to work out your answers.

☐

Challenge 3 The table shows the journey time of four trains leaving Station A
and arriving at Station B. Work out the lengths of the train journeys.

	Station A	Station B
Train 1	10:55	12:20
Train 2	11:30	1:45
Train 3	12:40	2:30
Train 4	1:55	4:30

a Write the journey times of each train.

Train 1 ☐ : ☐   Train 2 ☐ : ☐

Train 3 ☐ : ☐   Train 4 ☐ : ☐

b Which train has the longest journey? ☐

c Which train has the shortest journey? ☐

d What is the difference in time between the
shortest journey and the longest journey? ☐

e Train 5 left Station A at 3:05. It arrived at
Station B 1 hour 45 minutes later. At
what time did the train arrive at the station? ☐

☹ 😐 ☺

223

Lesson 4: **Reading a calendar**

• Read a calendar and calculate intervals in weeks or days

You will need
• calendar

1 Find April on your calendar. Write the dates of all the Thursdays.

_____

_____

2 Use your calendar. Write the number of days in these months.

Month	Number of days	Month	Number of days
November		October	
May		March	
September		February	
January		June	

Which is the shortest month? _____

Use the calendar below to answer these questions.

Monday	Tuesday	Wednesday	Thursday	Friday	Saturday	Sunday
1	2	3	4	5	6	7
8	9	10	11	12	13	14
15	16	17	18	19	20	21
22	23	24	25	26	27	28
29	30	31				

1 Write the days of the week that these dates fall on.

    a 24th _____   **b** 6th _____

    c 13th _____   **d** 29th _____

2 Which months could the calendar page above be for?

_____

_____

3 How many days from the first Tuesday of the month until the second Friday? Show how you worked out your answer.

4 How many days between the second Wednesday of the month and the last Monday? Show how you worked out your answer.

Challenge 3

1 Use your calendar. Work out what dates are:

a 21 days after 24th April

b 6 weeks after 23rd June

c 4 weeks and 6 days after 1st November

d 18 days after 3rd March

2 Use your calendar. Work out what dates are:

a 12 days before 11th July

b 5 weeks and 2 days before 12th December

c 28 days before 13th October

d 7 weeks and 5 days before 25th February

Lesson 1: **Charts and tables**

- Record information in charts and tables and interpret them

Challenge 1

1 This tally chart shows learners' favourite colours.

yellow	𝍸 𝍸 |||
blue	𝍸 𝍸 𝍸 𝍸
red	𝍸 𝍸 𝍸 ||
brown	𝍸 |||

a How many learners like:

blue ☐ red ☐

yellow ☐ brown ☐

b How many learners took part in the vote? ☐

2 Complete the table to show the information from the tally chart in Question 1.

Colour	**Number**

1 This tally chart shows the number of different fruits sold on a market stall.

Fruit	Number
papaya	⊞⊞⊞ ///
watermelon	⊞⊞⊞
kiwi fruit	⊞⊞⊞⊞⊞⊞
pomegranate	⊞⊞ //
mango	⊞⊞⊞⊞ ////

a What are the three most popular fruits?

_____

b Which is the least popular fruit?

_____

c What is the total number of watermelon and kiwi fruit sold?

2 Represent the information from the tally chart in Question 1 in a table.

3 What is the difference between the number of mango and the number of pomegranate?

227

Handling data

Handling data

1 There are:

- 36 learners in Stage 1

- 28 learners in Stage 2

- 35 learners in Stage 3

- 29 learners in Stage 4

- 32 learners in Stage 5

- 34 learners in Stage 6

a Show this information in a tally chart.

b Show the information in a frequency table.

2 Make up three statements from your table.

_____

_____

_____

Handling data

Lesson 2: **Pictograms**

You will need
• squared paper

• Show and describe information on a pictogram

This tally chart shows learners' favourite fruit. Show this information as a pictogram on squared paper. Choose your own symbol. Each symbol should represent 1 learner.

Favourite fruits	
mango	~~HHH~~ ~~HHH~~ /
apple	~~HHH~~ ///
kiwi	~~HHH~~ /
banana	~~HHH~~ ~~HHH~~

1 Look at the pictogram and answer the questions.

a How many more green than brown sweets are there?

b How many orange and red sweets are there altogether?

c How many more yellow than purple sweets are there?

d How many sweets altogether?

Colour	Number of sweets
green	● ● ● ◖
orange	● ● ● ●
blue	● ● ◖
pink	● ● ●
yellow	● ● ● ● ◖
red	● ● ● ●
purple	● ● ● ◖
brown	● ◖

Key ● = 2 sweets

2 The table shows some learners' favourite wild animals.

Animal	Number of learners	Animal	Number of learners
elephant	12	buffalo	9
lion	14	lemur	15
gorilla	10	tiger	21

Draw a pictogram to show this information on squared paper. Each symbol should represent 2 learners.

Challenge 3

1 a Write down five sports in the space below. Read out each one and ask the class to raise their hands to show which is their favourite. Count how many and record the results as frequency table. Your teacher will give you some paper.

b Now show the information in a pictogram on squared paper.

c Use the information in your frequency table and pictogram to make up four questions.

_____

_____

_____

_____

☹ 😐 ☺

231

Lesson 3: **Bar charts**

- Show and describe information on a bar chart

You will need
- squared paper

1 This table shows learners' favourite sports. Show the information as a bar chart on squared paper. The intervals should be in divisions of one.

Favourite sports	
Sport	**Number of learners**
football	12
basketball	8
swimming	6
gymnastics	5

2 Look at your bar chart from Question 1. Write down three pieces of information that your bar chart shows.

_____

_____

_____

1 Look at this bar chart, then answer the questions.

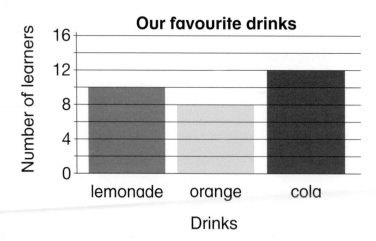

a How many more learners like cola than orange?

b How many learners in total voted for lemonade and orange?

c How many were asked altogether?

2 The table shows some musical instruments played by learners. Represent this information on a bar chart on squared paper. Intervals should be in divisions of two.

Instruments played	
Instrument	**Number of learners**
drum	20
piano	15
guitar	24
violin	10
recorder	9

a How many more learners play piano than violin?

b How many fewer learners play recorder than guitar?

 1 Describe how a pictogram and bar chart are the same.

_____

_____

_____

2 Describe how a pictogram and bar chart are different.

_____

_____

_____

3 This frequency table shows sports that a group of learners like.

Sports our class like	
Sport	**Frequency**
football	20
rugby	12
swimming	24
baseball	15
tennis	16

a Put this information into a pictogram on squared paper.
Use one symbol to represent two learners.

b Now put the information into a bar chart on squared paper.
Mark the frequency axis in steps of 2.

c Write five statements you can read from the information.

_____

_____

_____

_____

_____

Lesson 4: **Venn diagrams**

• Use a Venn diagram to sort data and objects

 Challenge 1 Write what is the same and what is different about cats and children in this Venn diagram.

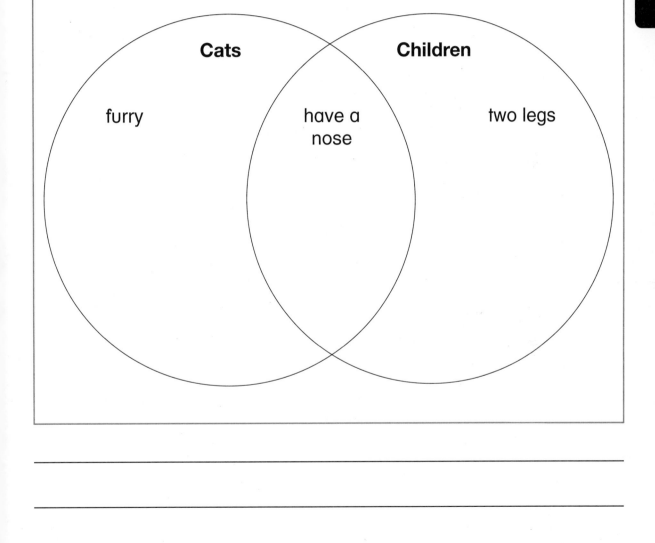

Cats   **Children**

furry   have a
          nose   two legs

_____

_____

_____

_____

☹ 😐 ☺

Challenge 2

1 Draw a circle, semi-circle, triangle, square and pentagon in the correct places on the Venn diagram.

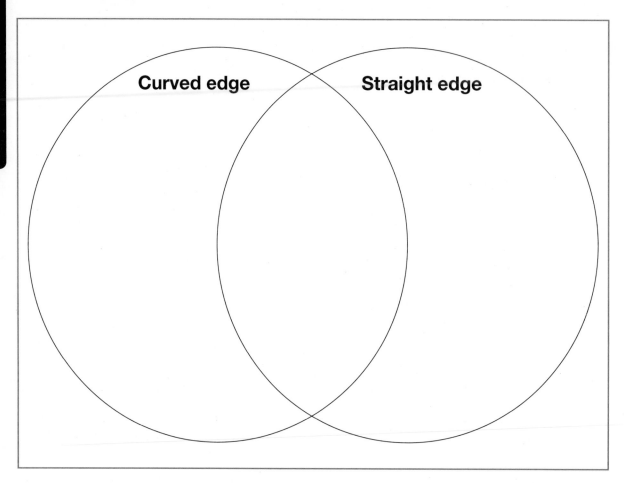

Curved edge   **Straight edge**

2 Write three statements from your Venn diagram.

_____

_____

_____

3 Jocelyn drew a Venn diagram. She could not understand why there were no numbers in the middle section.

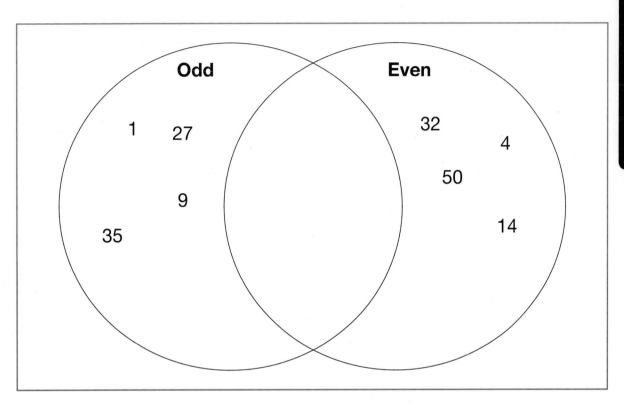

Explain why Jocelyn cannot put any numbers in the middle.

_____

_____

_____

_____

Challenge 3 Look at the Venn diagram.

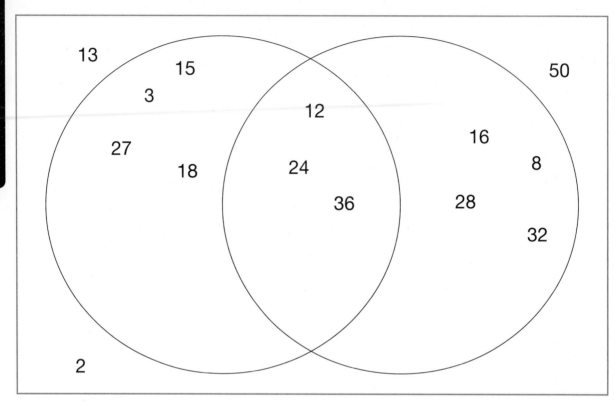

What could be the criteria for this Venn diagram?

_____

_____

_____

_____

_____

Lesson 5: **Carroll diagrams**

• Use a Carroll diagram to sort data and objects

Challenge 1

Write or draw the shapes into the correct part of this Carroll diagram.

4 sides or less	Not 4 sides or less

circle
semi-circle
triangle
square
rectangle
pentagon
hexagon

Challenge 2

1 Write the numbers in the correct places on the Carroll diagram.

6   8   27   19   16   35   36   45

Then, add three more numbers to each section.

	Even number	Not even number
Multiple of 3		
Not multiple of 3		

☹ 😐 ☺

2 Write three statements from your Carroll diagram.

_____

_____

_____

3 Benjamin drew a Carroll diagram. He could not understand why there were no numbers in two of the sections. Explain why this is.

	Odd	Not odd
Multiple of 2		4, 10, 20, 36
Not a multiple of 2	5, 13, 27, 33	

_____

_____

_____

_____

_____

3

1 Look at this Carroll diagram.

	56, 168	49, 84
	24, 72	23, 55

What could be the criteria for this Carroll diagram? Write them in to the diagram and explain your answer below.

_____

_____

_____

_____

_____

2 Write two more numbers to each of the four sections on the Carroll diagram.

241

Lesson 6: **Using charts and tables**

- Collect, organise and interpret data using tally charts and frequency tables

You will need
- squared paper

1 Sam wants to bake two types of biscuits to sell at the school fair.
Look at the tally chart.
The chart shows how many he sold last time.
Which two types of biscuit should he bake?

vanilla	ЖЖ ЖЖ /
chocolate	ЖЖ ЖЖ ////
chocolate chip	ЖЖ ЖЖ ЖЖ //
almond	ЖЖ ЖЖ ЖЖ
butterscotch	ЖЖ ЖЖ /

_____

_____

2 Chef wants to put a new main course on his menu. He asked his customers which courses they would like him to add.
Look at the table. Which new course should he add?

_____

Main course	Number of votes
Steak and cheesy mash	36
Salmon fish cakes and chunky chips	28
Pasta surprise	37
Vegetable supreme with rice	25

3 Explain why you made your choice.

_____

_____

Challenge 2

1 Interview 20 people. Collect the data and record tallies in the table below.

When is your birthday?	
January	
February	
March	
April	
May	
June	
July	
August	
September	
October	
November	
December	

2 Use the data to create a frequency chart on squared paper.

3 Write two statements about your data.

_____

_____

Challenge 3

1 Measure the height of 16 different people to the nearest centimetre. Record your data here.

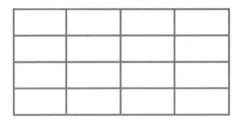

2 Choose a suitable range, for example go up in steps of 5 cms: 80–85 cm, 86–90 cm, and so on.

3 Use the data to create a frequency chart on squared paper.

4 Write two statements about your data. _____

_____

_____

243

Handling data

Lesson 7: **Using pictograms and bar charts**

- Collect, organise and interpret data using pictograms and bar charts

You will need

- ruler
- squared paper

This table shows part of the medal table for the 2012 Olympics.

Use the data to create a pictogram on squared paper.

Country	Number of gold medals
Jamaica	4
Kazakhstan	7
Brazil	3
Kenya	2
China	38
France	11

Challenge 2

1 Go outside and record the number of different types of transport that you see in 10 minutes.

Type of transport	Frequency

2 Use your data to create either a bar chart or a pictogram on squared paper.

3 Write two statements about your data.

1 Survey 15 people to find out what they think about recycling. Think of six questions that have a yes or no answer. The first one has been done for you as an example.

Question	Yes	No
Should we have can recycling bins in school?		

2 Organise your data into two bar charts, one for 'Yes' and one for 'No' on squared paper.

3 Compare your bar charts and write four statements about your data.

_____

_____

_____

_____

Lesson 8: **Using Venn and Carroll diagrams**

You will need

• Resource sheet 25: Carroll diagram template
• Resource sheet 30: Venn diagram template

• Collect, organise and interpret data using Venn and Carroll diagrams

1 A music teacher wanted to organise either a recorder or a percussion club. Look at this Carroll diagram.

	Recorder	Not recorder
Percussion	12	25
Not percussion	20	8

a Which club should she organise?

_____

b Explain why.

_____

2 Henri wanted to know which fruit to give his class at snack time. The learners gave him this Venn diagram of their choices:

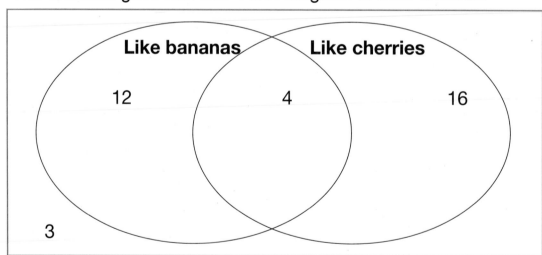

Write this information on the Carroll diagram below.

	Bananas	Not bananas
Cherries		
Not cherries		

3 Which fruit should Henri provide the most of?

_____

4 How many bananas should he provide?

_____

5 Will all the learners be provided with a snack if Henri provides bananas and cherries? Explain your answer.

_____

_____

Challenge 2

1 Interview 5 girls and 5 boys. Collect the data and record it in the table below.

Name	Girl/ Boy	Age	Favourite colour	Number of letters in first name	Has a bicycle	Can swim

☹ 😐 ☺

2 Use the data you have collected to sort the names into this Carroll diagram.

	Can swim	Cannot swim
Favourite colour is green		
Favourite colour is not green		

3 Use the data you have collected to sort the names into this Venn diagram.

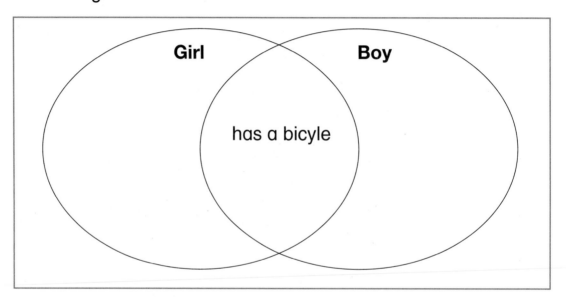

Girl   Boy

has a bicyle

Challenge 3

1 Use the data you have collected to create a Carroll diagram with two criteria using the Carroll diagram template.

2 Use the data you have collected to create a Venn diagram with two criteria using the Venn diagram template.

3 Write four statements about your data.

_____

_____

_____

_____

Notes

Notes

Notes

Notes

Notes

Notes